John Bluck is a writer and broadcaster with a lifetime of working on bicultural issues. His earlier books include *Wai Karekare: Turbulent Waters*, *Hidden Country: Having Faith in Aotearoa*, *Killing us Softly: Challenging the Kiwi Culture of Complaint* and *Seeking the Centre: Living Well in Aotearoa*. A retired Anglican bishop, and Dean of Christchurch Cathedral before it fell down, he has worked ecumenically all around New Zealand and overseas, serving as Communication Director for the World Council of Churches in Geneva. He lives with his wife Liz in Pakiri, north of Auckland, where he writes, gardens, and tries to catch fish and play the trumpet.

BECOMING PĀKEHĀ

JOHN BLUCK

HarperCollins*Publishers*

HarperCollins*Publishers*
Australia • Brazil • Canada • France • Germany • Holland • India
Italy • Japan • Mexico • New Zealand • Poland • Spain • Sweden
Switzerland • United Kingdom • United States of America

First published in 2022
by HarperCollins*Publishers* (New Zealand) Limited
Unit D1, 63 Apollo Drive, Rosedale, Auckland 0632, New Zealand
harpercollins.co.nz

A catalogue record for this book is available from the National Library of New Zealand

ISBN 978 1 7755 4210 0 (pbk)
ISBN 978 1 7754 9241 2 (ebook)

Cover design by Hazel Lam, HarperCollins Design Studio
Typeset in Adobe Garamond Pro by Kirby Jones
Printed and bound in Australia by McPherson's Printing Group

MIX
Paper from
responsible sources
FSC® C001695

Contents

Preface   1

Introduction   5

PART I

NŪHAKA TO PAKIRI:

WALKING BETWEEN TWO CULTURES   11

  1 The way New Zealand used to be   13

  2 We'll make a man out of you   29

  3 The Canterbury brand   36

  4 Into the cauldron   44

  5 This country ain't what it used to be   49

  6 Living between the headlines   58

  7 Dreaming of rainbows   70

  8 It's alright here   75

  9 Cracks in the Gothic   86

10 Finding the thin places   105

11 Becoming a retiring Pākehā   120

PART II

WHERE WE ARE   131

12 The inflammatory debate   133

13 Trying to talk to each other   141

14 Invisibility's fine – subscribe to mine   146

15 Call me by my name   160

16 Do Pākehā need protocols?   173

17 Promises, promises   181

18 Would you drive a hybrid?   192

PART III

WAYS AHEAD   203

19   That's what friends are for   205

20   The two of us   210

21   Shared stories that won't let us go   229

22   Biculturalism built in   246

PART IV

FINDING A SHARED FUTURE   263

23   The landscape has shifted   265

24   Aotearoa as it just might be   276

Bibliography   291

Acknowledgements   296

Preface

This is a book I've long been trying not to write. It ought to be easy, but it's not. I began under the cover of a pseudonym, for fear some friends will read it and won't stay friends. Well, that's too bad. It has to be a personal story, as it is for many other unsettled Pākehā who relish the privilege of living here and have spent a lifetime trying to belong in this land. That should be easy to do. But it seems to get harder and is often uncomfortable, as Kiwi film makers keep showing us through what Sam Neill called their 'cinema of unease'. Home, yet still an alien place.

Some Māori might respond, 'That's too bad for you, mate, because for us it's often not only uncomfortable but destructive and deadly. We bear the brunt of a history you created for us.' I can only say, 'I'm sorry about that, but we're facing up to that right now, and we know we have to, because, as Pākehā, that's our history too.'

It's a strange, strange landscape that we live in. Beautiful, green though sadly not so clean, a haven rather than a hermit kingdom at the world's end that makers of fantasy films flock to because it can so easily be made to look enchanted, as our tourism posters did for a century.

But the common space Pākehā share with Māori is volatile and often fraught. When Pākehā do connect with te ao Māori, the Māori world, by being escorted onto a marae, watching the haka at the start of an All Black Test, listening to a kapa haka performance, laughing with Taika Waititi or simply being caught up in the chords and melodies of 'Poi E', especially when they're far from home, many stop and wonder. Why is this unfamiliar Māori world so disconcerting and affecting? How has it become so much part of them, however little of it they understand? Māori living in New Zealand have no choice about being bicultural. They have to operate in what is still a dominantly Pākehā world. Pākehā don't have to. They can still live here as though Māori don't exist.

This is a book about the discomfort of being Pākehā; how they might live with that, get used to wearing the name until they find a better one, learn to laugh about it, and even to relax and enjoy it. As the title suggests, being Pākehā is a work in progress. The word carries freight they weren't aware of 50 and 100 years ago. And as the debates about colonisation and rangatiratanga heat up, so the meaning of Pākehā is refocused and sharpened. Definitions once trotted out so confidently look quaint in retrospect, even slightly silly. I'll look at some of that history of becoming Pākehā, the romantic ideas and failed models of bicultural harmony, and celebrate some success stories. And I'll do that knowing that what I write now will quickly be outdated as the bicultural journey accelerates.

And let's be very clear about the terminology. The temptation to reach for a multicultural story over the top of the bicultural one has become popular, and understandably so. After all, there are more Chinese or Indian New Zealanders than there are Māori, so it makes sense to say, 'Let's get on with enjoying that diversity and making it work.' Of course this country's future will be multicultural – more cultures are added by the year – but I firmly believe that we need to first establish a just relationship between the original two. If Māori are the first culture of this land, then Pākehā are the second, and with that comes a special responsibility. No future will ever work if we get there by forgetting how we began as a nation, honouring the promises Māori and Pākehā made to each other in 1840 and redressing the mistakes made since. None of what I have to say will reach those determined to insulate themselves from the cultural volcanoes that surround us, but if you sense that there's still some unfinished business to becoming a New Zealand where Māori and Pākehā can co-exist, and are both the better for being alongside each other and sometimes even together, then this might be the book for you.

It's also for those New Zealanders who may not be comfortable about calling themselves Pākehā, and are open to exploring why that's so, but are also bothered by the way in which Pākehā and Māori talk about and to each other. Bothered, if not bewildered, and often not a little sad and angry.

Introduction

Is the way Māori and Pākehā interact worse than ever? Well, it's certainly more heated, and is that a bad thing? Much worse is that they increasingly don't talk *to* each other; and in that silence, there's a storm brewing. How did we get into this mess? After more than 200 years of co-existence under the umbrella of a treaty unique among colonised countries, you might think things would be better. Despite some better recent news from education and health statistics, progress is uneven and frequently contradicted by new evidence of racism, poverty and historical abuse. It feels more like a journey of one step forward and two steps back.

Māori visibility in the media and public life is certainly greater than ever before. You can't watch a rugby or netball match without being reminded of that (though you'd hardly know from watching cricket, tennis or surf lifesaving). Lisa Carrington, our most famous Olympian, is of Te Aitanga-ā-Mahaki and Ngāti Porou descent. But personal contact is another matter. Pākehā and Māori worlds grow ever more separate, in silos defined by wealth and the lack of it.

Just as the elderly get cordoned off into retirement homes, so Māori and Pasifika people are gathered into the lowest paid jobs, the lowest decile schools, the lowest quality (though still high rent) housing. On the streets of any suburb that is even moderately wealthy, and in the schools, cafés and shopping centres that serve them, Māori are pretty much invisible. In our biggest city, the presence of newer New Zealanders is much more obvious. On the streets of our southern towns and cities, Māori are hard to find. They attend a disproportionate number of our decile one schools.

And that invisibility is an obstacle for Pākehā understanding of the depth and urgency of Māori calls for respect and self-determination. Māori are four times more likely than Pākehā to end up in jail and have, on average, a life expectancy that's 10 years shorter. And, unlike the stereotype of perpetrator, they're eight times more likely to be a victim of crime. Their chances of owning a home have fallen by more than 20 per cent over the last 40 years. Their deprivation is rooted in inequality.

When a society allows its citizens to become distanced by income and everything that flows from that gap, such as access to education, healthcare and decision-making, the absence of brown faces becomes familiar and normal. Sometimes that gap is deliberately maintained, by landlords who turn away Māori tenants, and employers who avoid hiring Māori workers, and health and education planners who assume that one size fits all. Most of the time, though, it's a matter of institutionalising that invisibility. Sorry, says the system, it's just the way things are.

And I don't think that's orchestrated by some evil cabal of white supremacists. It's the inevitable outcome of market forces and the lingering legacy of our colonial history. So Pākehā shouldn't be surprised that Māori become more critical and angry as their understanding of inequity becomes clearer.

Māori will increasingly take charge of their own destiny. It's already happening with the creation of an independent Māori health authority, the development of a school history curriculum that tries to embrace the conflicting sides of our story, the reform of Oranga Tamariki and the justice system, co-ownership and governance of businesses and institutions, and management covenants of parks and rivers. The list is expanding and the momentum is unstoppable.

But equity, let alone equality, for Māori will never be restored in Aotearoa without better ways of talking to and about each other. Māori and Pākehā have yet to find a mutually respectful partnership, and it's hard to achieve in the current climate where each side demonises the other with labels like greedy, rapacious, guilty, ungrateful, privileged or, worst of all, resorts to plain indifference or cowed silence.

There has to be a way out of this impasse. It won't be found by demanding that Pākehā go home; or by expecting that Māori will gradually disappear, as so many believed a century ago; or that, having survived, they just blend in, as government policy required in the 1950s. Nor will it happen by Pākehā simply giving up their wealth. The way ahead will have to be negotiated more carefully than by issuing ultimatums, however angry

Māori are about their dispossession. And there will need to be new signs of good faith from Pākehā, in the form of owning a history that requires repentance as well as pride, attempting to understand how different Māori knowledge and language is from what Pākehā take for granted, and letting go some habits that continue to insult and demean. But the first step is some more honest conversation among Pākehā about what good partnership requires of them and looking at how they might be getting in the way of that wider dialogue with Māori.

The current climate makes this conversation especially fraught, thanks to the culture wars that rage around the globe and spill over into Aotearoa. Andrew Anthony has reflected on why these cultural conflicts have become so much sharper. He lists the declining trust in institutions that were meant to hold us together, the growing inequalities of wealth and privilege and, most of all, the spread of technology that encourages people to cluster only in their self-selected, like-minded groups. All of this, he argues, shifts public focus towards symbolic and emotive issues that are packaged together into ideological job lots. Platforms like Facebook and Twitter feed on name calling, point scoring and virtue signalling. The battle lines become more moral than political, with demarcation not so much between left and right as right and wrong. And Donald Trump added to that inflammatory climate by rewriting the public discourse rulebook and practising a new rhetoric of rage and well-honed abuse.

That's the international climate that frames our local debates and widens the divisions between us. We paint ourselves on a global canvas. Māori are supported by alliances of indigenous peoples worldwide and the protection of United Nations conventions. Pākehā observe the dismembering of their European colonial heritages around the world and look on, bewildered, as the statues start toppling here.

So let's start this search for a better way of talking to each other, and adding a little flesh to the bones of this identity I'll call Pākehā for the moment. I write as a white man and as a layperson, without any special expertise in race relations. I've dipped into the huge pool of academic literature and specialised scientific reports on this subject, and sometimes risked drowning in it. I'm simply a journalist at heart, trying to access the knowledge that Māori and Pākehā need to live graciously and justly with each other in Aotearoa. Let's begin with the story of my own lifelong journey from one Māori village to another, with lots of stopovers in between.

PART I

NŪHAKA TO PAKIRI: WALKING BETWEEN TWO CULTURES

CHAPTER 1

The way New Zealand used to be

It was a hot day in Nūhaka in 1954 and the annual rugby match between the primary school and the native school had barely begun. Already I wanted the dreaded event to be over. There was nothing I could add to the proud tradition of Nūhaka rugby with its All Black luminaries like George Nepia. As a skinny white kid in the front row of the sweaty, muddy, head-scrunching scrum, nothing but ritual humiliation awaited me. The 'native' team was bigger, heavier, stronger, hugely more accomplished and better led. Their teacher, Hui Matiu, was legendary for his high-volume, passionate coaching style. People would come to listen and watch him, as much as his team. His players dared not fail and the score against us ran into silly figures. Worse still, coming from a school with such a small roll, I'd probably have to play prop again next year. But maybe I'd be dead by then, or have run away. And as it turned out, I did. Off to Napier to stay with Grandma and go to a school where rugby wasn't compulsory, or even very important.

* * *

Nūhaka today is best known nationally as the best place to view space launches from, across the bay at the Rocket Lab base in Mahia. Drive down Blucks Road (I'm proud to say), walk over to the beach, look left and marvel. We didn't marvel much about anything in Nūhaka, a small settlement on Highway 2 between Gisborne and Wairoa, but we were glad to be there. My dad used to tell me there wasn't a better place to be in the whole world. And, like most of the other men, both Pākehā and Māori, and a few women, recently returned from a war in Europe and the Pacific, he meant that literally.

I thought it was pretty good as well. We lived on the edge of a river where we swam and fished and canoed, with a big garden where we built forts, dug tunnels and, armed with slug guns, replayed the battles depicted in our favourite *Battler Britton* comics. Bikes were our most prized possession. My grandfather bought me a brand-new Raleigh with three speed gears – a state-of-the-art model that few other kids in the village had seen, not Pākehā and certainly not Māori, though I didn't think about that at the time.

The Education Board school just up the road, oddly and ambiguously known as the public school, had two teachers and 30 to 40 children, all Pākehā. The native school, as it was called, across the river, had 10 staff and around 300 children. Rugby matches aside, we were worlds apart. Yet there was no sense of the separation being hostile; in some areas there was no separation. Nearly all the drivers who worked in my father's trucking business were Māori and I treated them like uncles, heading off on trips with them to collect wool and hay bales, sheep and cattle, and loads of shingle from the quarry on Blucks Road. They taught me words and told stories I never heard at home. And the language exchanged between Dad and the drivers in the shed where he serviced the trucks was colourful and mutually abusive, but rarely offensive. Men in the 1950s showed their affection for one other by insults more often than compliments.

The transport company, as well as the dairy factory, railway station, service station and shops, along with local farms, supplied enough employment to sustain a thriving local economy for both races. Other institutions ran more separately, especially the several local women's groups. They didn't exclude Māori but I don't remember seeing any as members of the Country Women's Institute or the Garden Circle. The Country Library branch, which operated out of our washhouse, had only a handful of Māori borrowers and I don't recall any of them being asked to join the elite team of book pickers allowed to choose titles during the mobile library van's infrequent visits.

The shops, and there were several – two general stores, a butcher, a saddlery, a bakery and a post office – though Pākehā owned, were seemingly happily integrated places. They must have been, since Johnstone's General Store down the road had a barrel of salted mutton birds on the steps. I can still gag at the smell on a hot summer's day. I doubt there were many Pākehā customers. But it all seemed to work for both cultures, unless you ran out of credit at the store and were refused service, much to the embarrassment of everyone present. I say 'seemed', because my child's eye view of all this was uncritical and accepting. We lived in a world within two worlds, rubbing up against one other but rarely melding, let alone meddling. And when we did, it was always clear to me, without being told, that Māori ran this place. Perhaps my rugby experience was more of a parable than I realised.

The local church scene didn't fit this pattern. There were Presbyterians of both races, served by a long-established mission; Catholics, whose nearest church was in Wairoa and seemed very exotic; and Rātana, whose presence was whispered as numerous but never seen (hardly surprising, as they'd been excommunicated by Anglican bishops back in 1928 for being too fond of angels and prophecies). Equally mysterious but much more visible, and sharing those same fondnesses, were the Mormons. The Church of Jesus Christ of Latter-day Saints had been working in New Zealand since 1854 and was well established in the Māori world, but unlike the Anglican church, was unscarred by the disastrous consequences of involvement in the land wars of the 1860s. The Mormons had funded and built, with local labour, a modern chapel in Nūhaka. It was the largest building in town, with a carpark big enough for a fleet of vehicles, but as far as I knew, no one in the Pākehā community had ever visited. When asked why it was so big, the elders explained that they were building for the future, for all of us.

The Mormons had also built the proudest building in the village, the Rākaipaaka War Memorial Marae, opened by Peter Fraser in 1949. It was a beautiful space and a showpiece of traditional carving by the master craftsmen Pine and Hone Taiapa. Anzac Day services were held there, Māori and Pākehā standing together in a building that commanded awe and respect from all of us, sharing the losses from a war whose scars were still raw. (Fifty years later we returned to the marae when my daughter's short film was shown at the Māori Film Festival there. It was a lovely reconnection.)

Two worlds, side by side but sometimes touching. Not in the food we ate. For Pākehā it was a very *Edmond's Cookery Book*-based cuisine. I never tasted fried bread or a boil-up. Puha was never served at home. We ate fish but not the heads, crayfish but not the yellow custard inside the skull. And I never learnt to enjoy kina or fermented corn.

But the two worlds did touch regularly in the Anglican church, where the Pākehā vicar came only monthly but the Māori pastorate priest presided every week. The liturgy and hymns were in te reo and though we didn't understand the words, we knew we were welcome. The lay reader from the Māori pastorate, a tall, dignified man in an elegant black cassock, helped to teach us Sunday school. One Sunday he collapsed in our midst, writhing on the church floor with an epileptic fit. As children ignorant of such things, we were all terrified, not knowing what to do. To this day, the plaque on the church wall in his memory gives me pause and adds to the respect in which I hold this bicultural building.

Church was one of the very few places where I remember hearing te reo spoken. It was not taught or spoken in either of the schools, or by the drivers in the trucks I rode around in. There were elders who kept the language alive on local marae but in the workaday world of Nūhaka, te reo was hard to hear and officially discouraged, even punished at school, though that policy was unevenly applied. Back before the First World War, English was the language used at the native school, but the grammatical principles of Māori language were also taught. It was claimed that local Pākehā taxi driver Jimmy Pearson had learnt to speak it fluently in order to manage difficult clients.

As Pākehā, we happily pronounced Nūhaka as 'Newhawker' with no fear of correction. My brother Richard, who is 12 years younger than me, was a junior pupil in 1962, after the two schools had amalgamated, and the cultural landscape had shifted. He remembers, as a six-year-old, struggling to pronounce correctly the name of his new teacher, Mrs Hana Whaanga, who had a 40-year career at the school. The story went that she forbade inspectors from entering her classroom unless they spoke Māori. She knew our family well, but we had happily mispronounced her name for years. Richard's embarrassment stays with him to this day. That new era of cultural awareness was also brokered by some Pākehā. The school principal during Richard's time was a Norwegian teacher named Johan Bonnevie, who promoted te reo and waiata, along with a mixture of classical music.

The Mormons may have built chapels and halls but much more important for a nine-year-old was the LDS Theatre they owned and ran as a movie house under the steely-eyed caretaker, Ponti Te Kauru. Armed with a long torch, he would patrol the upstairs and downstairs seating areas to keep order. When the audience grew unruly or threw ice creams at the screen downstairs, or rolled Jaffas down between the seats upstairs, Ponti would stop the projector until calm returned.

The Mormon owners wouldn't have approved of all the movies we saw there, or of the Māori kids being downstairs and the Pākehā upstairs. The segregation, never named or enforced, was bridged only by the smell of pies heating in the snack bar, which wafted up and down the stairs, ready for half-time sales that everyone enjoyed, along with a soft drink called Green River and a cigarette outside if you were old (or discreet) enough.

As Pākehā children we rarely visited Māori homes or had Māori friends or visitors in ours. When we did, they more often talked to my parents in the back porch, and once in a while at the kitchen table. I remember a driver and accomplished clarinet player, whom I begged to give me lessons, meeting me in the driveway to deliver a music book, but reluctant to come into the house. I was upset by his hesitation.

Surveys through the 1950s showed Pākehā attitudes to 'mixed marriages' were mostly negative, though more for daughters than sons, but such relationships were commonplace in Nūhaka. An uncle of mine had fathered a Māori daughter years before but it was never spoken about in the family. My own parents' attitude to Māori was positive and open. My mother had Māori women friends and struggled with te reo classes for much of her life, continuing to learn the language into her nineties. But I remember the shock of their refusal to allow me to take a teenage Māori girl I'd met to the movies. Many years later I discovered she was a cousin, the daughter of my uncle's not so secret child. Some Pākehā families, though not ours, were wary about their daughters marrying a Māori. It would mean being absorbed into their whānau, having to share possessions, take care of relatives and look after everyone.

New Zealanders were keen moviegoers in those years, and there was plenty of drama on the screen, but little of it was indigenous, even though there had been a very modest local industry since 1896, mainly documentaries, many involving Māori themes, such as the long-lost 1901 production, *Māori Canoe Race at Ngaruawahia*. Perhaps this might even have been screened in Nūhaka, for my grandfather had a movie theatre running in the village before the First World War: Bluck's Pioneer Picture Show it was called. I still have one of the original glass advertising slides, which reads, 'In front all the time: watch out for the *Hunchback of Notre Dame*.' The country's first feature film, in 1914, was called *Hinemoa*, its most famous, in those early years, Rudall Hayward's *Rewi's Last Stand* in 1925.

The homegrown movie industry took a great leap forward in 1952 with John O'Shea and Roger Mirams' *Broken Barrier*, which broke new ground with a bicultural love story set in nearby Mahia, where the young Pākehā bloke arrived to woo his Māori beloved, alighting outside the general store from a Bluck's Transport bus. That might have been the reason my father was interested in taking me to see it at the Opoutama Hall. It was a revelatory experience for me, seeing our faces in our places on the big screen, telling a love story that was reenacted in Nūhaka every day. The movie's impact was as much geographical as it was about character and story. Much later filmmaker Gaylene Preston talked about film making 'an already beautiful landscape articulate'. Somehow Nūhaka, as reflected in this movie, embedded its bicultural story as profoundly as any words.

Buildings, too, held bicultural stories. In the 1950s we knew Te Kotahitanga Marae at Whangape as the Unity Hall – kotahitanga means unity or solidarity – venue for dances and the annual fancy dress ball, where, for a night, we would pretend to be fighter pilots and princesses, kings and queens (but only of the English kind), highwaymen and cowboys and cowgirls. Nobody ever dressed up as a Māori chief. In 2017 Ngaire Aben-Tuhiwai took over the building as a site for extended education, offering tutoring and support for local kids adrift from formal schooling and needing to complete their NCEA credits.

Then there were the memorial monuments outside its doors. One commemorates Ngāti Rākaipaaka chief Īhaka Whaanga, familiar from the famous Gottfried Lindauer portrait, who supported local Pākehā settlers and land sales in the 1850s and fought against Pai Mārire forces in the 1860s and was involved in the hunt for Te Kooti in Te Urewera. Another memorial nearby honours the six members of the Nūhaka Women's Hockey Team, Māori and Pākehā, who died together in a bus crash in May 1947, shocking a community still reeling from the losses of the Second World War.

There were two bridges in town. The Nūhaka River bridge divided the village between the mostly Māori west side and the mostly Pākehā east. Māori boys dived off the railings into the snag-prone water far below. Our parents considered that incredibly dangerous and strictly forbidden, but we secretly envied the divers, admiring their courage, but never daring to try. The Wai (Waikokopu) Creek bridge was a favourite spot for eeling from at night. You would throw your slimy catch up onto the bridge, hoping a car wouldn't come along as you did so. One memorable night, an eel flipped through the open window of a vehicle and into the face of a well-known local Māori identity. He talked to our parents, we were punished and the repercussions for race relations in the village took weeks to resolve.

The roads were all still shingled and dusty in the 1950s, often dangerously prone to floods and slips that closed access for weeks. Every corner told a story of near misses and accidents, often fatal. The most storied section of road, for both Māori and Pākehā communities, ran from Nūhaka to the nearest pub in Mōrere, three miles away. Drink driving in the 1950s was more of a cultivated skill than a crime. As children we'd hear those crashes talked about as though they were normal.

On the surface Nūhaka seemed a happy place. As our school textbook *Our Nation's Story* told us, the Treaty of Waitangi 'remained the fairest treaty ever made between Europeans and a native race; indeed in many ways, it was much fairer to brown man than to white'. That was enough to reassure me for the next

20 years. But beneath the surface lay some snags. Although no one in Nūhaka used that word, and the Hunn Report which endorsed it was still a decade away, assimilation was the policy of the day: Pākehā expected Māori to become more and more like them. In Nūhaka we Pākehā kids knew Māori were different, but not always, and some were similar enough to us to pose no surprise, even no threat (except on the rugby field). It seemed to us that Māori, especially the kids, didn't mind acting, dressing, playing and learning like Pākehā. We were growing closer. It was only a matter of time.

* * *

To boys like me, much of what was really happening under the surface in Nūhaka was unnoticed or only hinted at. And there were plenty of hints. Like the attitudes to land ownership. I remember Pākehā farmers complaining about how hard it was to acquire land from Māori because of their shared ownership and multiple titles and their reluctance to sell. We could get rid of the blackberry and farm it much more productively, was a common refrain. But no one explained to me what it must feel like to be a people who once claimed the whole country, all 66 million acres, almost 27 million hectares, of it, and now controlled only six million, and over 100 years had lost legal control of their collective land titles. Some of that lost land was legitimately sold but overwhelmingly it was confiscated or fraudulently traded. There was also the strong underlying suggestion that Māori farmers weren't as smart as Pākehā ones, despite evidence of successful dairy herds all around the village run by Māori, and some dodgy farming operations run by Pākehā.

Equally unformed were our attitudes to local poverty and the systemic reasons behind it. I don't remember seeing anyone going hungry – everyone had large gardens and fish was plentiful – but the houses in which some large Māori families had to live were pretty basic. Kids commonly went barefoot summer and winter but warm clothes were often in short supply. And some roads in the poorest areas were to be avoided when out bike riding, my sister tells me, though they were okay for boys. Poverty was a problem that could be solved by trying harder. Not that we had to. Although there were few luxuries in our house, I had the sense we were still privileged.

Violence was a less hidden feature of Nūhaka culture. The war had finished only a decade before and left its crippling aftermath in the lives of returned soldiers and the children and wives they had to get to know over again. Domestic violence was visible but publicly ignored. I remember a woman neighbour who would often have to go shopping with a bruised face. No one said a word. Drunkenness was common but again not paraded, except for the cars that ran off the road coming back from the Mōrere pub. There were stories of soldiers, both Māori and Pākehā, who stayed drunk for weeks on their return from overseas and took months to recover.

Matenga (Jack) Rangi Papuni, who has explored the toll taken by the Second World War on the spirituality of Māori soldiers, paints a sobering picture of those who came back. (Many didn't. Of the men who served in the 28th Māori Battalion, three-quarters were killed, wounded or imprisoned and reported missing.) Papuni describes vividly the pain and suffering that 'could be seen in their faces and on their bodies. Some struggled with feelings of hopelessness, a lack of purpose in life.' This loss of wairua or spirit played out in alcohol abuse, violence, post-traumatic stress and withdrawal. The dynamics of all that were rarely addressed or understood, even by the veterans' own community, and certainly not by young Pākehā boys.

Violence permeated life in the 1950s. Rugby was basic and brutal. Fights broke out at Nūhaka club matches, with spectators joining in. Once the game was closed down when the referee had to be escorted away after a decision the crowd didn't like. I don't remember physical fights beyond the playground variety, but there were chilling stories of high school kids in savage altercations on their way to Wairoa College. The school bus driver would stop en route and tip the scrapping students out to finish their brawling on the roadside. To be a man in Nūhaka meant standing up for yourself and behaving by the rules. Bad behaviour had a physical cost. Boys were strapped for it. Criminals were hanged. Eight were executed during my primary school years; in 1955 alone, four died in Mount Eden.

Curiously, the presence of firearms didn't seem to accelerate or even endorse that violence. Nūhaka was a well-armed village. Licences weren't required and we graduated from air rifles used to shoot birds and the porcelain insulators on telephone poles, to .22 rifles, 410- and 12-gauge shotguns to shoot ducks, pūkeko and rabbits, and .303s to shoot deer and pigs. Target shooting on local ranges was a popular sport; a trophy from the Nūhaka Rifle Club was a much-respected prize.

None of these activities, with either bullets or fists, was racially defined or divisive. Māori weren't seen to be more or less violent than Pākehā. Gangs were yet to arrive in the village. As a boy growing up I felt as physically safe and comfortable with either racial group. We enjoyed the unrestrained freedom of the whole village, both east and west of the river, by day and by night, when we went eeling and possum shooting in the dark. My sister reminds me that girls didn't enjoy quite the same freedom. Codes of proper behaviour, largely unspoken, constrained the games girls could play, the bad words they could say, the families they could be with, the clothes they could respectably wear. I can't think of a better place to begin a life, for reasons that it's taken me a lifetime to distill. It gave me the chance to know how to live as a minority group, surrounded by an indigenous culture that welcomed you; and, more privileged though you were, tolerated your ignorance and bewilderment about them, and allowed you to work out a way of co-existing, and sometimes thriving together.

Yet so much of that life we shared back then I still don't know much about. What did Māori kids my age say when Selwyn Toogood asked them, as he asked me every week on the radio show *It's in the Bag*, 'What's he going to do, New Zealand?' Did they wonder as fearfully as I did what would be revealed when, in a lonely room above the Thames, Major Gregory Keen would turn another page in the radio serial *Dossier on Demetrius*?

I know they were as enthralled as I was by the cowboy and Indian serials at the Saturday movies, though did they have more than a sneaking sympathy for the Indians? They certainly enjoyed the main features, such as *The Dam Busters*, as much as I did because I heard them yell in delight when the bouncing bombs were dropped. And at the annual Nūhaka A&P show, there was no separation in our love for candy floss and sideshows, dodgems and roundabouts. Māori and Pākehā were defined by the same brand names and labels, attached to the same ice creams and trucks.

Years later I wrote a poem about it, which included these lines:

> *Bedfords back then were the truck of choice*
> *The best of British, no Jap stuff, said the drivers at the R.S.A.*
> * (though the mechanics whispered otherwise).*
> *Everything you drove and wore had a provenance of pride*
> *Viyella shirted, sport coated in Harris tweed and if you had*
> * an acre or two, a green felt hat. Raincoats were elegant*
> * gabardine, or oilskin, military serge lingered and Levis*
> * hadn't arrived.*
> *Women's heads were hatted and under their dresses, corsets and*
> * stays (mystery word to a five-year-old). You could feel the*
> * bumps and ridges of this scaffolding inside the embrace of*
> * elderly aunts*
> *And everyone sported pins, badges and blazer pockets boasting*
> * prizes, memberships and royal approvals, or more simply,*
> * highly commended proficiency*

in fire lighting, first aid and bicycle maintenance.
It was a world of loyalties never flouted, certainties never
  doubted,
and an underlying order to a world so badly wrecked by wars
that God could not possibly ever allow them to happen again …

And the music that we heard from radio hit parades and dance bands at the Unity Hall, more often than not led by Māori musicians, came from the States but were given an Aotearoa twist. (There were rare home-grown exceptions like 'Blue Smoke' by Ruru Karaitiana.) For instance, we loved to listen to Hank Williams' 'Jambalaya (On the Bayou)'. It's about a Creole rice dish eaten in the swamps of Lousiana but when John Reo played it on sax in the Unity Hall, it was pure Nūhaka, through and through.

CHAPTER 2

We'll make a man out of you

He was a new boy like me, anxious, shy and afraid of what boarding school in Napier would hold, away from home for the first time. But, unlike me, who could ease my bouts of homesickness with a three-hour trip back to Nūhaka, George was in exile, fresh off the boat and weeks away from Rarotonga. I remember how desperately he missed home. On our Friday afternoon leave he would take me with him to the house of his parents' friends who had lived in Rarotonga for years. Their home was full of homesick-easing photographic memories, colourful tivaevae quilts, island melodies and exotic fruits like coconut and mango, all of which intrigued me with their foreignness.

* * *

Napier Boys' High in the 1960s had few Māori or Pasifika students, and those who did come, left early. George stood out as 'other', a reminder of a world outside my own and a wake-up call to just how white the school was. We became friends. He came home with me for holidays and went on to establish himself as a leader in the school, and later in the medical profession. He was the first of many 'others' in my life, people who stood out by not fitting in, not only because of the colour of their skin, but, even more importantly, because of their way of seeing the world, their anger at injustice, their hunger for a better way. Sometimes they stayed in my memory because of the struggles they had to face and the alienation they had to carry as travellers through foreign territory. By simply being around them, I was compelled to question everything I took for granted.

The book presented as a prize for public speaking in my final year at high school summed it up. Charles Dickens' *The Tale of Two Cities* begins, famously, 'It was the best of times, it was the worst of times', and so it was for me, and maybe George as well, though I haven't spoken to him for over half a century. Worst of times because the boarding school was a brutal place, shaped by a post-war macho white culture, hard drinking and rugby playing, all the time reassuring itself that everything was sweet. Unsurprisingly, boys tried to emulate that, just as we emulated our fathers by dressing exactly like them.

Forty years later I was invited to speak at the school's annual prizegiving and present more books, though Dickens didn't feature this time. I told the boys that back then there were no prizes for the things that would have been most valuable to me: fluency in te reo, the ability to choose a good partner, to understand climate change and conservation science; skills to critique economics, religion and politics, film and television, to say what was wrong about the *Holmes Show* apart from the fact that he went to Hastings Boys' High, and to have even a basic knowledge of the local history that shaped the region. I learnt all about the wars and kings of England but no word on the kings of Waikato and fighting with Pai Mārire that happened in the hills behind the school.

Teenagers and youth culture were still being invented, and boys were in a hurry to be ready to go to war again. We expected that to happen, so it made sense to have an armoury next to the classrooms, full of .303's and Bren guns. The official story was they were only for practice by cadets and shooting teams but we suspected something more was going on. Who knew when an enemy might turn up? A much later movie called *Red Dawn* would prove us right: communists invade a small American town and the well-armed local school cadets hold them off. We would have loved that film in 1961.

We left school knowing that what a man had to do, a boy had to do even sooner. Men drank beer and women drank Pimm's. Men got jobs and stayed in them, not flash but steady work. Women could too, but didn't have to. Boys could dream about doing something different from, even better than, their father but it was okay if they didn't. Better to do the same, but bigger. Some wit listed the probable careers of my final year classmates – farm worker, deer culler, barman, market gardener and, for me, truck driver. The farm-linked jobs were the best as we still lived in a subsidised paradise. A farmer neighbour named his fishing boat *Rebait* because he'd bought it, effectively, with a tax-break grant. The only drugs we'd heard of were aspros. Sex of any sort was a subject of mystery and terror.

* * *

The best of times at high school in the late 1950s came when we'd finally crept our way up the seniority ladder above the bullying, fagging, savage caning and humiliation of junior years. Up in the rarefied air of the lower and upper sixth form, life was full of privilege, reward and opportunity. The letters and articles in the school magazine were confident, earnest, optimistic expressions of how lucky we were. But there wasn't a hint of anything Māori. The bicultural story that had formed me back in Nūhaka disappeared without trace, except for George's ever-present reminder of 'otherness' – and even he was blending into the white woodwork. A letter he wrote to the magazine took the form of a Shakespearean speech, tongue in cheek but very English in affectation.

There were Māori students at Napier, and even Māori heroes and role models. Our head prefect, Teddy Bennett, was literally a rock star of a leader: sportsman, singer and guitarist with his own hit records to boot. His group, Teddy and the Bears, went on to make three hit singles but back in 1961 we all knew the words to his song 'Let's All Twist Tonight'. And there were other Māori leaders from famous Ngāti Porou families, like the Koheres and Reedys, who were stand-out figures. Amster Reedy, named after Amsterdam where his father fought in the Second

World War, went on to become a noted academic and kaumatua leader of three Olympic Games teams.

But, despite being exceptional young men, these were exceptions in the monocultural world of Napier Boys' High. When I look back through photos of sports teams, classes, arts and music productions, brown faces are hard to find. And the staff were all Pākehā. Nūhaka felt a long way away and the Māori world I'd known there faded quietly into the background of my very white life.

* * *

Women of both races were still taking back seats in the late 1950s. A controlling male, macho culture was still in place and well cultivated in boarding schools like Napier. Given the education we received about women, or more correctly the education we invented for each other, it's a small miracle that any of us managed anything approaching a healthy sexual relationship, let alone a good marriage. Our understanding of the female body and psyche, whispered in the dark in late-night dormitory conversations, was bizarre beyond belief.

Homosexuality was treated equally exotically, and left to be explored in the homoerotically confined spaces of rugby scrums. That was the only place where physical touch was sanctioned. Gestures of affection and friendship were seen as girly or queer. Violent touching, on the other hand, was okay, under the control of teachers and housemasters who caned with bamboo rods, sometimes until we bled. Most masters did this reluctantly and sparingly, others frequently for the silliest infringements, whole classes and dormitories at a time. And a few caned sadistically with seeming pleasure, and zero accountability. We would go to sleep at night in the dormitory next to the master's study, to the sound of punishment inflicted. To call out or cry was unacceptable. You kept your pain and terror to yourself. This culture of sanctioned violence, male privilege and control defined Māori as readily as Pākehā.

The late 1950s and early 1960s saw a seismic cultural shift for Pākehā but the timeline of key historic events records astonishingly few Māori landmarks. The first Waitangi Day celebrations began in 1960 but they won few headlines and aroused little controversy. Kiri Te Kanawa's career was launched by winning the Mobil Song Contest in 1965 but the coronation of the first Māori Queen, Te Atairangikaahu, a year later passed me by. Much later I read about the Save Manapouri Campaign in 1969, a huge environmental movement triggered by plans to raise the levels of Lakes Manapouri and Te Anau to provide power for Comalco. Ten per cent of the population signed a petition in protest. Six guardians of the lakes were later appointed, all Pākehā men.

The assimilation policies that shaped us in the 1950s were dug in deeper than ever through the 1960s, an era famous for its upheavals in music, manners, food and fashion. When the Beatles toured in 1964 and I waved to them on the balcony of the Clarendon Hotel in Christchurch, I thought I'd joined the sharp edge of the swinging sixties. But the much bigger cultural revolution that would hit New Zealand in the 1970s was still well hidden from Pākehā eyes. The protest movement that began after the All Blacks toured South Africa in 1960 without Māori players, in order to satisfy the terms of the apartheid government, would grow and produce endless confrontations that built to the bloodshed of the 1981 Springbok tour. But as a young student, finishing high school and on my way to university in Canterbury, immersed in an increasingly purely Pākehā world, all that passed me by. A ferry trip to Christchurch in 1962 was to change all that.

CHAPTER 3

The Canterbury brand

In those days, the interisland ferry went overnight from Wellington to Lyttelton. You slept in multi-berth cabins with no say in who you shared with. That was okay for a calm crossing, but on a rough one the smell of vomit could be overpowering. One of my cabin mates was Hone Kaa, a short, stocky Māori from Rangitukia, north-east of Ruatoria. We were about the same age, got talking and found we were both from the East Coast, both headed for Christchurch. Without wanting to be pushy – he wasn't that forthcoming – I asked some more questions. It turned out we were both enrolled at College House, an Anglican hall of residence, to study for an arts degree and begin training for ordination to the priesthood. And when we got to College House, we found we'd been assigned to share a room for a year. So began a lifelong friendship with a man who, more than anyone else, welcomed me into and guided me through the Māori world, nudging, laughing, calling me all sorts of names as I stumbled along.

* * *

Life at College House and the University of Canterbury was liberating after five tightly monitored years at Napier Boys' High. I couldn't now how much fun a young man on a motorbike could have in a city which, back in the 1960s, was incredibly tolerant of students. Hone often rode pillion behind me on my 350cc Velocette, a machine not made for two of our size. We should have been killed several times.

Hone lived more dangerously than I did, his romantic adventures much braver than mine. Our shared room had a sash window that opened onto the street, which enabled him to make early-morning entries unnoticed. Hone got away with things I'd never dare to try, but as long as we were not late for chapel, especially the Compline service at 9.30 each Saturday night, no one seemed to mind.

I watched his reception into the life of the 'House', as we called it, with great interest. Hone was the only Māori student, apart from one other who preferred not to identify as Māori, much to Hone's bewilderment. Many of the students, mostly from Canterbury, had never met a Māori and were fascinated by him, in the way you are with a previously unencountered wild creature. Looking back, I can't help but recall the accounts of tattooed chiefs who accompanied missionaries on trips back to England in the 1840s, drawing admiration and awe from fashionable Victorian society. Not so fashionable Canterbury society behaved similarly with Hone. The quote describing him in the College House magazine (attaching quotes to names was a favourite pastime) read, 'O little brown brother, are you awake in the dark?'

Hone tolerated the curiosity with good humour and enjoyed playing up to the stereotypes. His career peaked as star performer in the capping revue show, where he relished the role of Hōne Heke chopping down the flagpole at Russell. As the week of performances rolled on, adherence to the script, carefully vetted and formally approved by the vice-chancellor, got looser and the references more phallic. Hone didn't return to the House the following year. Examiners deemed him not academic enough and he went on to St John's College in Auckland to prepare for ordination. Later he would earn a doctorate and become a respected teacher and scholar. Canterbury had enjoyed him but didn't know how to accommodate him.

That short-lived partnership aside, my student life in Canterbury was a journey through an all-white world, oblivious to the long history and presence of Ngāi Tahu. It was as though the South Island had popped out of the sea and remained empty until the English settlers landed. The south knew more about moa than about Māori, who featured in tourist posters, amid glaciers, hot pools and cabbage trees. One of my jobs through the long university summer holidays was to work as a courier for Trans Tours: up to 10 days on a bus around the South Island, looking after the passengers who were largely Australian nurses and teachers and retired British tourists. My role was to provide a commentary over the intercom. I researched these spiels assiduously and could talk for hours about the history and geography of whatever rolled past the bus windows. But I can't remember ever mentioning anything to do with Māori.

As has happened so often through my life, my education in things Māori went on hold for a few years. It was replaced by a crash course in Pākehā culture of the hard-nosed, tightly bound and parochial Canterbury brand. There is no one size fits all in the Māori world and the same applies to Pākehā. College House, formerly the upper department of the private Christ's College, was an incubator unit for the cultivation of this all-white Canterbury culture. Most of us were from single-sex boys' schools so our understanding of women was still primitive. The House magazine told stories like these, thought by us at the time to be hilarious:

How can you get a meal at Connon? [The women's residential hall nearby] *Put your name down and pay 3 shillings.* 3 shillings! I wouldn't pay 3 shillings for a Sunday tea at Connon. *You're paying for sex as well.*

And then for variation:

Why don't you go out with girls more often? *Oh, I prefer the chaps at the hostel.*

I've left out the names on these cringeworthy stories. The men involved are now prominent figures in science and engineering and probably wouldn't enjoy being reminded of them.

Pākehā culture, Canterbury style, was hard to break into, and once you did, by attending somewhere like College

House, or dating a girl from St Margaret's in Christchurch or Craighead in Timaru, or playing some hard-knuckled rugby, then there were rules to follow. Look after your mates. Respect your traditions. Even go to church, but not too often. Be polite when you're sober. Rules don't apply when drunk. Dress for the occasion. Be punctual. One friend from a high country farming family had always dressed for dinner (black tie) at home to sit down to the leg of mutton. It was no surprise to him, as it was to me, that College House required the wearing of ties, sports coats and academic gowns for the evening meal and chapel services.

An editorial in the House magazine spelt out this code of Pākehā conduct. On belief: 'This is a Christian college … therefore no one can rightly live here and refuse to worship.' This was followed by, in bold type: 'If anyone can't subscribe to the beliefs and practices of this place then obviously he is here under false pretences, and therefore should get out.' An antiquarian typeface was used for the courtesy section: 'At House meetings it is a duty and a privilege to be present … the same applies to the privilege of sitting at Top Table. Discourtesy through lateness has been a feature of both, the supreme insult being given during the House Ball when some groups arrived very late.'

The same editorial's advice on 'crossing the threshold to maturity' capped it all: 'Some never make it. Learning to live life urbanely is rather like a young girl's struggles with make-up: at first the effect is usually over or underdone and extreme. With time this mellows, though some women continue garishly for the rest of their lives, just as some men may drink, smoke and have sex excessively. At University we are learning to apply the adult cosmetics of beer, sex, religion etc. and … may go to extremes before we find the particular blend that suits the complexion of our personality.'

No one would dare to hand down such advice today. It is as unthinkingly prescriptive and smug as any protocol written for a Victorian drawing room; and as earnest and middle aged, though aimed at very young men. And for all its detail, there is no mention of anything Māori, or Pākehā for that matter, because the assumption is that everyone thinks like us and needs to act like us to be acceptable. In all the many places I have lived and worked, I have never encountered another cultural template so clear and confident and so effective at moulding and shaping lives.

I certainly soaked up the confidence it gave us and the permission to have a go at anything. In capping week, the city authorities allowed us to smash up old pianos in Cathedral Square, sit atop poles for days in Hagley Park, seal off roads, ride down the Avon riverbed on bikes … Pulling off such stunts without being locked up left us feeling pretty special. It was all great fun and a perfect seed bed for sprouting a sense of entitlement.

My cultural adjustment also extended into the lecture theatre. Canterbury's English Department was pioneering the study of New Zealand literature, still emerging from the earlier era of cultural cringe about anything from here. My master's thesis was on the works of Frank Sargeson and the anti-Puritan theme in his writing, and I had to read widely among other New Zealand authors. But not a single Māori name, and there were several notables to choose from, featured on my reading and assignment lists. We knew nothing of *Te Ao Hou/The New World*, the bilingual journal founded in 1952 that promoted Māori writers and poets, and had never heard of Patricia Grace, Hirini Mead, J.C. Sturm or Rowley Habib.

Nor did the movies, which provided the bulk of our cultural and entertainment diet, do much to help my bicultural awareness. The homegrown screen production was pretty limited, fed mainly by government-backed tourism promotions like *Amazing New Zealand* (1964), a light-hearted romp across boiling lakes, geysers, golf courses and toheroa-stocked beaches, then later *C'mon to New Zealand* (1969) and *This is New Zealand*, made for Expo '70 in Osaka. They date badly, especially *Holiday for Susan* (1962), which promoted the country as destination for adventurous young women with such lines as 'Women don't take fishing seriously but they'll enjoy it just the same.'

We were much more interested in the allegorical classics from Sweden, Britain's Cold War spies, kitchen sink dramas and Hollywood Westerns. John O'Shea's *Runaway* in 1964, which I can't recall very vividly especially since it was in black and white, was nothing like as powerful as *Broken Barrier* a decade before. *Runaway* was the story of a dodgy accountant on the run, who met up with a young Māori woman played by Kiri Te Kanawa. It featured the screen debuts of Selwyn Muru, Barry Crump and Ray Columbus.

The only dent in this almost completely white surface of my life came with holiday jobs back home, driving trucks for my dad. I dropped back easily into the banter and camaraderie and weathered the jokes about abandoning Nūhaka. 'Weren't we good enough for ya?' they asked, without malice or any real expectation of an answer. But that only served to make it clear I had left home for good and there was no returning.

I departed from Canterbury after five happy, challenging years, hugely more confident than when I arrived with Hone. He had gone on to be ordained as a priest and begin parish work. Our lives and our pathways grew apart. My own patience with the church was diminishing, even though I was still an ordination candidate in training. The very Church of England constraints concerning its language and liturgy, theology and practice felt very wrong to me. The expression of anything indigenous, whether Pākehā or Māori, was stifling and my work in New Zealand literature only heightened that sense. The further training on offer at St John's College in Auckland seemed more like an English monastery than a meeting house fit for purpose in Aotearoa, though it had been founded to be just that. I decided to look further afield, to the United States, much to the anger of the St John's College board, who had generously given me a scholarship through my Canterbury years.

CHAPTER 4

Into the cauldron

He was a Boston cop in the badged blue uniform and distinctive hat that, until then, had only been the stuff of movies and TV. But there he was, blocking my path out of the airport, the first handgun I'd ever seen in an open holster on his belt, demanding to know what I was carrying over my arm. Why did he pick on me? My hair was much longer then, as were my sideburns. Perhaps he thought I was a drug mule, an agitator, a draft dodger. In the midst of the Vietnam War there were plenty of them, though enrolling in a seminary gave you a 4F exemption card. 'It's a cassock, officer,' I said nervously, careful to use the title I'd heard on TV. 'I'm on my way to a seminary.' He looked at me with a mixture of disdain and disbelief. Kids who looked like me didn't go to any seminary he'd ever seen in Cardinal Cushing's archdiocese. He frisked me expertly, dug deep into the cassock pockets expecting to find a joint, then shook his head and told me to get on my way.

*　*　*

Despite the familiarity fostered by hours of watching American TV and movies, ordinary life in Cambridge, Massachusetts, in 1967 still felt strange. People said hi and welcome and good to see you, even when you'd hardly met them. They told you how they felt as soon as they met you, sooner by a year or two than anyone ever did in New Zealand. And friendships were made ten times faster.

It was a white world I lived in, as a graduate student at Episcopal Theological School (ETS). Adjoining the Harvard campus, it was part of a network of similar schools, Catholic and Protestant, that taught the same degree. We were mostly very white, but a small group of Black students were exploring a student culture of their own after generations of being absorbed and ignored.

Compared with the racial tensions beginning to grow in New Zealand, the American scene was already red hot and about to become incendiary. The civil rights movement was well advanced. At the doorway to the school chapel stood a monument to Jonathan Daniels, a white ETS student who had been shot and killed in Alabama a year before while working as a volunteer for a Black voter registration campaign. He was a martyr in our midst, a reminder of how high the stakes were in this battle for equality and equity. I quickly learnt the difference between those two words. Without equity, the balancing of resources, equality remains a noble but distant ideal.

In Cambridge, there was the Black Manifesto, a campaign for reparations to be paid to the Black communities for the generational damage done by slavery 100 years before. The campaign gained ground at ETS. As the editor of the campus newspaper, I often wrote about it. To raise funds, our campaign focused on selling a huge and expensive Persian carpet that covered the sanctuary floor in the chapel. The students agitated. The trustees wouldn't budge. Later, Liz and I were married standing on the same carpet. I learnt some things about how far and how slowly institutions can shift the cultures that created them.

The three years in Cambridge were constantly framed by racial politics woven into the anti-war movement that was played out with a passion and intensity I'd never encountered at home. Hearing the speeches of Martin Luther King, live in the Boston Garden Stadium and constantly on television, being in the crowd at Grant Park in Chicago during the Democratic Convention where police rioted against the student protesters, hearing the riot squads practise their chants and shield-banging manoeuvres outside our apartment building, all served to scare me into seeing how racial injustice was a life or death issue. Working to end it could be deadly.

And it was all very close up. Liz nursed at Mount Auburn Hospital, where her patients included veteran policemen suffering heart attacks and injuries sustained in riot control. Although they didn't bring their firearms into the ward, they often hid a blackjack under their pillow, accustomed as they were to living fearfully.

And it could get very personal. One early morning a fire broke out in one of the apartments in our building. We stumbled out down the stairs, banging on neighbouring doors as we made a dash for the street. Once clear we checked who was there, only to find a Black family missing. They soon emerged, unscathed, and looked at us accusingly. 'Why didn't you wake us too?' they asked? We started to defend ourselves with explanations before realising that nothing we said was going to be believed.

The lines between races, occupations, students and the working stiffs who resented their privilege, ran like deep rivers through Boston life. As an outsider I was able to cross those rivers in ways my white American friends often couldn't, simply because I didn't fit the racial and cultural stereotypes. I made friends with Black families through local churches I worked in, dated a Black woman and enjoyed the freedom I could enjoy by being an 'other' with a funny foreign accent. I learnt about the tribalism that divides Boston – Black and white, Jewish, Catholic and Protestant – into neighbourhoods separated from each other as surely as if by barbed wire fences. At the end of my studies I worked as a junior reporter on the Boston Catholic newspaper, the first Protestant to be hired. I'm sure my 'other' status helped.

Because most of the Boston workforce in police, fire service, ambulance and airport services were Catholic, I had privileged access to stories other media would never get. One assignment was to produce a feature on a day in the life of an air traffic controller. I walked into the entrance hall of the same airport I had arrived at three years before, confident this time that I was an insider, nodding at the cop on duty as though I'd known him forever. We both worked for the same tribe now. The controller

I interviewed couldn't have been more forthcoming. It happened to be the day the first Boeing 747 he'd ever seen landed in Boston. Together we watched the giant aircraft float down onto the tarmac. 'Holy hell,' he said. 'That ain't a plane. It's a fuckin' hotel.' When you're inside the tent you get to hear everything.

Soon after that experience Liz and I headed back to New Zealand, unaware of how the country had changed during our absence. Maybe the racial revolution I'd been living through in the States hadn't made any impact. Maybe our island tribes were still well insulated from the upheavals that the rest of the world was undergoing.

That looked to be the case as we waited in Air New Zealand's departure lounge at Los Angeles, ready to fly out. The passengers, all Pākehā, looked and spoke exactly as we remembered. An older man in a bowling club blazer with his white shirt collar turned out over the lapel. A young woman reading a copy of the *New Zealand Woman's Weekly*. Where did she find that? There was a bloke in a Swanndri, and a woman peeling an apple for her granddaughter. I hadn't seen anyone peel an apple neatly like that, the skin in one long coil, for three years. I was home already.

CHAPTER 5

This country ain't what it used to be

She arrived unannounced at the door of the vicarage in Kaiti in Gisborne, at breakfast time, fresh off the Road Services bus from Tikitiki, to welcome us home. We had just returned from living in the States, having to quickly find our way through the bicultural complications of this most Māori of towns. Sophie Kaa, Hone's mother, had been sent by her son to sort us out and make sure we were okay. She brought with her a kete of purple Māori potatoes (delicious) and fermented corn (an acquired taste) and the offer to help if we needed it. After her visit all sorts of doors opened.

* * *

We had come home to a very different New Zealand. Yes, the 1960s claimed to be swinging, but the swing came from overseas. We borrowed the energy. But in the 1970s it was homegrown, youth led and erupting out of anger and rebellion at authority, convention and white privilege. As a young journalist, I delighted in recording the progress of this eruption, not only across the face of the church I worked for, but also over every institution. The youth group I began in Gisborne produced a community newspaper with stories that didn't appear in the local paper: the failings of Māori education, poor working conditions for temporary Fijian labourers, prison reform, prejudice experienced by the local Chinese community. The story that drew the greatest outcry addressed the discharge into the sea of blood and offal from the freezing works. The stream of discolouration could be seen clearly from the city beaches but no one seemed to be able to change it or to be that bothered by it. The works were a major source of Māori employment and a key part of the local economy. We were regarded as impertinent and naïve in our complaint. Thirty years later, the same story would surface again, this time driven by Māori clergy. The pollution of water and seafood had been a grievance simmering for decades on local marae, and the fuse lit in the 1970s finally ignited.

There was a bicultural dynamic at work here. The energy that drove the social changes of the 1970s was very much powered by the Māori renaissance, but there were lots of Pākehā allies involved, however young and culturally clumsy they might have been. The calls for recognition of the treaty, respect for self-determination/tino rangatiratanga, restoration of land and language were the fuels for these fires, but the blaze spilled over into other areas such as education, law and the justice system.

The authority of every institution was under question. Young people were asking why before they said yes to anything.

A youth magazine called *Moment*, which I edited, delighted in these questions, joining the 1970s rebel chorus for liberation from whatever was in the way. Tim Shadbolt's *Bullshit and Jellybeans* was a staple text, along with the *Little Red Schoolbook*, inspired by the work of liberation theologians and educators like Paulo Freire and Ivan Illich, calling for a moral and educational overhaul. *The Little White Book*, by Danish conservative Christian writer Johannes Facius, countered with a call for traditional conformity when it came to schooling, sex, drugs and rock'n'roll. In reply, *Moment* magazine published its own little red book promising advice on more than sex, school and contraception.

Moment also promoted a board game we invented called Mana – a simulation game for youth in a multiracial society. It was designed to force players into assuming unfamiliar and challenging roles, then asking them how they felt and what they'd learnt from the game. A roll of the dice could drop you into or out of prison, off to university, or a commune, or land you with a criminal record that would dog your career. The cards dealt to each player had instructions that now seem dated and racially and politically loaded:

A famous guru convinces you that the reason you are
having trouble with the police and other authorities is due
to the colour of your skin. You believe him and get very
bitter about it. Go back 3.

You learn the Māori language at university but don't know any Māoris who can speak it. Go forward 4.

You join the Young Nationals and have a swinging time at parties. Go forward 5.

You push someone on the nose who says, 'Listen I've got nothing against Islanders. It's just that …' You are charged with assault. Pay $200 to someone who is doing well in the game. Go back 4.

Your parents find out you are pregnant. They send you away to a distant relative and tell everyone you have gone to work in Auckland. Go back 3.

Mana was a very Pākehā game, a light-hearted and blinkered attempt to cope with the social turmoil that kept building throughout the decade as landmark legislation slowly gave the Treaty of Waitangi legal authority. The Race Relations Act, passed in 1971, prohibited discrimination on the grounds of race, nationality or ethnic origin and established the office of race relations conciliator: Sir Guy Powles was the first to fill that role. In 1973, on Waitangi Day, Prime Minister Norman Kirk was famously photographed at Waitangi itself walking hand in hand into the future with a young Māori boy. The image was in sharp contrast to the disruptions that Ngā Tamatoa had led there only two years before. Later in 1973, 6 February was officially recognised as a public holiday, though renamed New Zealand Day. In 1975, the same year that the Waitangi Tribunal was established, Te Rōpū Matakite o Aotearoa, 'Those with foresight', launched a land march from the Far North to Parliament, led by Whina Cooper, chanting 'Not one more acre' and gathering 60,000 signatures as it went. And two years later, in 1977, Ngāti Whātua began a 506-day campaign of protest at Bastion Point in Auckland that ended with scenes of white-helmeted police arresting over 200 people – images that evoked the land wars all over again. And from 1974, and escalating in 1976, the infamous dawn raids rolled out against Pasifika overstayers.

Through all this turmoil, I had the privileged role of observer as a journalist and broadcaster in a radio programme called *Morning Comment*, which preceded the news each weekday on what is now RNZ National. The day after the overstayer raids began in Auckland, I had this to say about what Immigration Minister Frank Gill assured us was not at all about 'tracking, hunting or raiding them' but what the *New Zealand Herald* headline described as an 'Overstayer Blitz'. 'A brown face,' I said, 'becomes a pretext for interrogation and the spate of arrests makes nonsense of claims that it is business as usual.' The raids started at the end of a week in which the New Zealand Manufacturers' Association had held its convention, at which one speaker warned members about 'the growing danger of racial tension in our industry'. As I put it, 'He suggested it might be wise to hang onto the overstayers that clearly everyone knew about but used as convenient.' I ended by saying, 'I hope to have a quiet weekend. And I hope the shame I feel as a white New Zealander echoes in the silence.'

There were many media voices trying to interpret these bicultural and multicultural eruptions through the 1970s. On

Morning Comment and *Sunday Supplement*, we enjoyed free rein; I don't ever remember being censored. Nor on television, where I shared a weekly slot called *Column Comment*, in which several of us took turns to critique the media coverage around the country.

A lot of that coverage was directed at the New Zealand Rugby Union, which kept raising the temperature of the race relations debate. After sending the All Blacks off to South Africa in 1970 with Māori players included as 'honorary whites', it bumbled its way through to another United Nations-defying tour in 1976, triggering the boycott of the Montreal Olympics that year by almost 30 nations, the majority of them African. The game back then was managed by good blokes, many of them farmers who had once played well themselves but had never grasped the volatile racial and political complexity of how the sport worked off the field. Rugby's ability to pretend it played on a colour-blind paddock continued until the showdowns of the 1981 tour, which tore apart families and communities, Māori and Pākehā.

No sport has come close to being as destructive or as promising for our bicultural future. Rugby has provided wonderful role models for Māori and Pākehā, who achieved great things together through times when such partnerships were hard to find. But rugby has also left us ashamed and demeaned as a bicultural country. The seeds of that dynamic were sown back in 1928, when George Nēpia, born in Wairoa, not far from Nūhaka, was left out of the team to South Africa on racial grounds.

* * *

Māori writers began their public careers in the 1970s. Witi Ihimaera was the first Māori author to publish a short story collection – *Pounamu, Pounamu* in 1972 – and the first to publish a novel, the award-winning *Tangi*, in 1973. Other *Te Ao Hou* contributors also had firsts in this decade. In 1975 Patricia Grace's *Waiariki* was the first short story collection by a Māori woman writer. In the same year, Heretaunga Pat Baker's *Behind the Tattooed Face* was the first historical novel by a Māori author. Such people led the way for a chorus of Māori and Pasifika writers and poets, and put an end to the era of Pākehā talking only to and about themselves.

In 1976 a television drama based on a Witi Ihimaera story broke new ground, foreshadowing the public outcry caused by the film of Alan Duff's *Once Were Warriors* two decades later. *Big Brother, Little Sister*, directed by Ian Mune, explored Māori alienation through broken families, domestic violence and an abusive father, as seen through the eyes of two children, Hema and his seven-year-old sister Janey. It had a profound impact, but many viewers, Māori included, complained that it reinforced negative stereotypes

Ihimaera's long-time advocacy for te ao Māori, the Māori world, and tino rangatiratanga has made him into an elder statesman for the cause. In a 1975 booklet he wrote while at the Ministry of Foreign Affairs, he spoke softly and optimistically about an earlier and rather different vision. 'Māori culture and pākehā culture are gradually merging, and a New Zealand culture is evolving in their place. This is what the New Zealander of tomorrow will inherit.' And then with a hint of foreknowledge about the turmoil that lay ahead, he concluded, 'His inheritance will not come easily. It is something which even he, perhaps, may have to continue to fight for.' Back then, I don't remember writing or talking about being Pākehā with any great confidence or clarity. More often Pākehā were busy pretending it didn't matter, or reacting to the chants of protesters calling for them to 'go home'.

There was another less heated level to this bicultural debate that engaged many more New Zealanders. Homegrown cinema was still mostly missing in action but television programmes were starting to flourish. *Pukemanu*, a timber town drama that ran over 1971 and 1972, and starred, among others, Ian Watkin, Pat Evison and Ernie Leonard, was a delight, with its Kiwi voices and accents, Māori and Pākehā and rugged blokes in Swanndris. *The Governor* series in 1977 was the most lavish New Zealand production to date, costing $10 million in today's money, and the most controversial. It offered an unflattering portrait of Governor George Grey and opened up some ugly angles on our colonial history.

Tangata Whenua, the six-part 1974 series written by Michael King, was another bicultural breakthrough, despite the complaints it triggered saying it should have been produced by Māori themselves. Michael and I shared an office in 1972 as tutors at the Wellington Polytech Journalism School. Fresh from the *Waikato Times*, he was already immersed in writing about Māori. *Moko*, on Māori tattooing in the twentieth century, was published that year. His biography of Te Puea Hērangi would follow in 1977. Michael's advocacy for Pākehā pride was a benchmark in our bicultural journey. His claim that Pākehā could rightfully claim to be indigenous alongside Māori, even though they had not been here for as long, and that their culture was 'not something foreign [but] a second indigenous culture', drew angry reaction but he persisted. His seminal 1985 work, *Being Pākehā*, helped to define the debate about Pākehā identity and move it out of its earlier defensive stance. Michael was willing to be critical of Māori, though he worked hard to consult carefully and build personal relationships with the people he wrote about. He felt he had earned the right to publish material he had carefully researched and consulted over with elders, winning their trust to use it. And he believed literature about Māori often romanticised them and glossed over the darker parts of their history. Few Pākehā authors since have been so critical.

CHAPTER 6

Living between
the headlines

After working alongside Michael King for a year in the capital, my journey between the cultures headed to Auckland, where I was appointed as editor of the New Zealand Methodist newspaper that in 1975 became *New Citizen*. An omen of the turbulence to come popped up, or out, as Liz and I drove proudly into Auckland along the state-of-the-art motorway for the first time in our Vauxhall Viva. To celebrate our arrival, our two-year-old son threw his drink bottle out the car window. Through the rear-vision mirror, I watched it bounce on the tarmac behind us. There was no slowing down or turning back. This was going to be a whole new start.

* * *

The board of the newspaper took a risk in appointing me, young and inexperienced as I was, not even a Methodist, to follow the very senior editor, Ian Harris, who watched my progress, without comment, from a distance. *New Citizen* was a free paper, 50,000 copies distributed nationally each fortnight, proudly bearing Methodism's social justice agenda. The incredibly supportive board included people like a young lawyer with a precarious legal aid practice called David Lange and veteran *Auckland Star* journalists Jack Leigh and Maurice Berry, whose loyalty I tested when I ran a cartoon depicting Robert Muldoon with pig's ears. Maurice rightly said a church paper should fight fair, and we tried hard to do that better.

My indiscretion didn't stop Muldoon from later granting me an interview. He declared his displeasure with the church his grandfather had come to New Zealand to serve as a missionary in the 1880s. Methodists were trying too hard to be different, he said, and lacked the 'fundamental strength' he admired in Roman Catholics. His grandfather wouldn't have been pleased with that. I found the interview daunting and wrote, 'His straightforward, cut the nonsense approach is really a highly sophisticated rhetorical style ... In short, Robert Muldoon is about as down to earth as a flying saucer.' For all his reputation as a belligerent and reactionary politician, Muldoon held some surprisingly open views, not least about Māori gangs. He had a close working relationship with Black Power – they visited his office and honoured him with a haka at his funeral. Swimming against the tide of anger expressed by Norman Kirk's slogan in the 1972 election campaign, 'We'll take the bikes off the bikies', Muldoon promoted work co-operatives, school tutoring, sporting and recreational programmes to work with rather than against the gangs. It was a pragmatic and bold bicultural initiative from the unlikeliest of sources.

New Citizen gave me a front seat for the turbulent show that Auckland played through the 1970s, and the paper tried to cover stories often ignored by other media. Dominican priest Emmett Devlin did an undercover story on the appalling conditions of Pasifika factory workers. We ran an exposé of the environmental effects of a Dow chemical plant in Taranaki producing 245T. We had inside coverage of the Peace Squadron's close-up encounters on the Waitemata with nuclear submarines direct from its founder and leader, George Armstrong. Reporter Geoff Dobson spent a weekend with Auckland's rough sleepers, and in a report that enraged many of my liberal clergy friends, and led to calls for my resignation, he wrote the inside story of an encounter group, then all the rage. A small group would meet for a non-stop weekend, led by a trainer, to get in touch with their feelings. Geoff wrote very frankly, revealing the free-for-all atmosphere and the emotional and sometimes physical risks people took. For many the Human Potential Movement, as it was known, was therapeutic and healing; for others it felt manipulative and unnerving; for a few it was destructive. The extreme end of the movement was seen in the Centrepoint Commune led by Bert Potter, which ended in prison sentences and tragedy.

The Human Potential Movement never attracted interest or respect from Māori. They found a more effective form of encounter in hui on marae. Encounter groups were captured in a white middle-class bubble, fitting perfectly the mood of Pākehā culture seekers: introspective, self-absorbed, disconnected from the hard edges of poverty and conflict, enormously optimistic and just a little naïve. The movement encouraged them to feel better by taking a voyage around themselves, rather than the wider world beyond. In the search for a just bicultural future, this was a cul-de-sac.

What kept me focused on that search were people like Hone Kaa, who by then had moved to Auckland. Our families spent time and holidayed together. He gave me access to parts of South Auckland I'd never have entered alone, including the night community patrols in which police and clergy worked together with young people. And he introduced me over the years to his wide circle of friends – Selwyn Muru, Ranginui Walker, Witi Ihimaera, Jenny Te Paa – and to his sister, Keri, and brother, Wi Kuki, who once interrupted me while I was standing in the sanctuary to preach and told me to get up into the pulpit and do it properly.

My debt to Hone is huge, not least for the partnership he and his wife Jane modelled. She was Pākehā without the slightest interest in becoming Māori and was often impatient and outspoken about her husband's mates and their behaviour. Hone was equally confident about who he was, and gracious with Pākehā who didn't understand his culture and expected him to be like them. I loved listening to them work out the differences between the two worlds they came from and delighted in the common ground they created for their friends to share.

Hone's friend Rua Rakena became a friend to me also. A minister who led the Māori Methodist Church, he was elected Methodist president in 1976 and at the end of his term wrote warmly and affirmingly in *New Citizen* of what he had found in his travels: 'continuing vitality, increasing participation, increasing recognition of the pluralistic, multi-cultural character of our society.' But there was a sting in the tail of his report. Our race relations, he wrote, 'are a disturbingly vulnerable and fragile area. A lifting of the veneer has exposed a hard core of racist beliefs that cannot be ignored ... Many of the reactions we've seen against concerned groups are only symptoms of a deeper illness.' He would turn up at our house on a Saturday morning when I was still asleep and sit on the end of my bed to sort me out on the issues of the day when I needed it, even when I didn't think I did. Especially on the art of speaking so you can be heard, rather than ranting about what's wrong with the world. He'd find something positive to say first, as he did in his report.

But even Rua's patience, gentle and slow to anger though he was, had its limit. In a major feature we ran in 1973 on racial stereotypes, he fired a warning shot across the bows of those who thought we were getting along nicely. 'Thankfully, in our day we are seeing the emergence of a Māori who refuses to have a pākehā determine his kind of Māoriness and the place he should occupy in society. He is literally fed up with the whole business of forever fitting into pākehā life. Of all the current signs this one undoubtedly has the most promising signs for our future.'

LIVING BETWEEN THE HEADLINES

In the same feature we sought comment on stereotypes from a range of Māori leaders, asking them to respond to the following description, carefully distilled from views widely held in the 1970s. It was safe to say that many, perhaps even most, Pākehā would have considered it accurate. (As everyone did then, we used 'he' throughout without a second thought.)

The Māori is by nature a warm and generous person. He has a happy go lucky approach to life, loves an excuse for a holiday and doesn't take responsibility like work and finance as seriously as pākehā. He is not really intellectual, usually leaves school early and does better at manual jobs like freezing worker or shearer or driving heavy machinery. His good physical condition helps him in games like rugby. He's a great fighter and makes a good soldier. Music and singing is his great love. He has a natural sense of rhythm and is good on the guitar. He likes bright colours too.

The Māori loves his children and favours large families. He also seems to have a lot of relatives about, especially older ones. His great sense of hospitality is part of his tribal heritage. His understanding of the law is different from the pākehā, simpler, often childlike. This gets him into trouble, especially his 'what's yours is mine' attitude.

He is inclined to be overweight. That's probably because he likes his beer and favours a diet of fatty foods. He is shy by nature but a good bloke when you get to know him. By and large he fits well into pākehā life.

Several Māori leaders graciously accepted our invitation to respond to this breathtakingly ignorant and insulting description, though it didn't seem like that then. As a Pākehā writer I reprint it now with some trepidation, but we all need to own where we've come from.

Mira Szasy, vice-president of the Māori Women's Welfare League/Te Rōpū Wāhine Māori Toko i te Ora, wrote in response:

This stereotype has done damage to both Māori and pākehā I think. For the pākehā it has prevented him from seeing Māori as he really is. [And] the Māori has been seeing the pākehā through a gauze curtain, as it were, seeing the movement of the figure but never hearing what he's saying, never knowing what he's thinking.

And the Māori has played up to this image. It's as though he has a cultural tendency to act out an image because it appears to please the pākehā. He puts on a mask which only serves to convince the pākehā that his stereotype was right.

But behind his mask, the Māori has failed to convey his real self – to say who he really is. The Māori has played up to the stereotype for so long now that he has begun to think it really does describe what he's like.

But now the shadows are beginning to clear. The Māori is starting to examine himself and drop the image and that's just as well, because the stereotype has been going on for far too long.

This stunning piece of analysis, as powerful as the day it first appeared in *New Citizen*, was matched by commentary from other leaders like academic and author Ranginui Walker and journalist, cartoonist and soon-to-be race relations conciliator Harry Dansey, who dismantled the stereotype line by line. But the most devastating response came from Tamati Reedy, senior lecturer at Auckland Teachers' Training College. In a few lines he put our earnest little journalistic project in its place:

I love to be seen as a warm and generous person.
Someone once said, 'Out, out brief candle?'
I apologise for the misquotes etc. etc.,
For I'm not intellectual enough to know
How to say it or what it means.
True! I love my children,
And our large family – those to come, those gone;
You see we belong to a Great Chain of Being;
We are the faces of the Past, Present and Future.
Sure I'm overweight, too.
Beer and kumara – what a diet!
My statistics do not portend longevity,
But – what a way to die!
Shy by nature and a good bloke – that's me!
I'm Hori with a half gallon jar;
Brown ale and pākehā life.
I've drunk to the full.
Excuse me – I must go places.

The last word went to Hone Kaa, who was asked to reverse the stereotyping and paint a picture of a typical Pākehā:

> The pākehā is greedy. If he gets anything, he won't share it
> with anyone else. He's never satisfied with what he's got and
> always wanting something more. Consequently, he always
> looks miserable.
>
> He's money hungry.
>
> He tends to lump all Māoris together in one block.
>
> He's fussy – about things which don't matter to Māori.
> Like what he eats, what he wears.
>
> The pākehā is nosey – if there's anything going on
> he wants to know all about it, find out exactly what's
> happening.
>
> He is ignorant – he won't learn anything about Māori
> customs and he tramples over everything the Māori considers
> to be most valuable – like burial grounds, and institutions
> like the tangi. He sees these things as a waste of time.
>
> Pākehā smell of B.O. a lot of the time.
>
> They are insensitive to things – they never cry at
> funerals.
>
> The pākehā will borrow anything of yours but won't lend
> you anything of his. If you borrow something of his without
> his knowledge, the first thing he'll do is call the cops.

The tone of the contributions to this feature, especially those of Tamati and Hone, taught me something about how to conduct the search for bicultural understanding. They were able to be harsh and funny, tongue in cheek and serious at the same time, willing to take risks with their rhetoric, offending sometimes but very clear that you had to bring people with you before you could convince them. I thought I knew that. *New Citizen* worked hard to be funny and entertaining. Cartoonist Darryl Kirby drew for us in almost every issue, Jim Hopkins ran a regular satirical column, I reviewed film and TV shows, we covered music festivals and featured some humorous stories. But despite those efforts to lighten things up, the tone of the paper kept tipping toward the earnest, sometimes righteous end of the scale because it reflected the tone of the times in Pākehā culture.

There were exceptions, of course. For example, the *Footrot Flats* comic strip by Murray Ball, which later blossomed into an animated movie, began in 1976 and was widely loved across both cultures. The characters that surrounded Wal and his Dog in the fictional town of Raupo included several Māori, notably Rangi, son of a local teacher and a freezing worker, who was a better rugby player than Wal and once considered skinning Dog to make a fur coat. And Rangi's cousin, Puti-Puti, complete with a boom box constantly playing on her shoulder, was a city slicker from Porirua who would come to visit. Ball's work skilfully skated around the stereotypes with little offence. I doubt if he'd get away with it today, given how much more volcanic the cultural landscape has become. Back then there was more room to move. The boundaries between Māori and Pākehā weren't monitored and policed quite as carefully. I think, though I'm guessing here, that we were a little slower to take offence with each other. At the time, Hone Kaa used to delight in telling the story of the Pākehā traffic cop who stopped a Māori motorist he suspected of drinking. He asked him to take a Breathalyser test, then said he'd have to come to the police station for a urine test. 'You can't do that,' said the motorist. 'You're not allowed to take the piss out of Māori.'

We were an earnest lot in the 1970s, out to save the world from racism, sexism, exploitation and injustice at home and in the developing world, which soon was renamed the Two-Thirds World, just to be sure we weren't accused of underestimating its size and importance. But in the early part of the decade, debate about racism, even more than sexism, had the sharpest edges. Programmes to help Pākehā come to terms with the arguments began to appear, with the National Council of Churches leading the work. In 1969 it set up a Church and Society Commission, led by its secretary, Gnanum Gnanasundaram. Their reports called for a rethink of what equal opportunity meant in New Zealand but spoke optimistically about the future. 'Race relations in New Zealand are good,' Gnanasundaram wrote in *New Citizen*, 'perhaps as good as any other part of the world.' The commission later reacted strongly to accusations that Māori were oppressed and dehumanised, lumped in with the treatment received by Indigenous Australians. The council soon followed with a national Programme Against Racism that worked with small groups, also involving Māori consultants to monitor progress. These sessions lifted Pākehā awareness considerably but sometimes created outrage from participants who felt insulted by anything resembling a charge of racism. It became an incendiary word, as it still is. Former New Plymouth mayor Andrew Judd would testify to that half a century on: he describes himself, after all his courageous work on awareness building, as still a 'recovering racist'.

The debate in the 1970s was forever volatile. It divided families, communities and churches and sporting clubs, constantly fed as it was by the politics of rugby and the on again, off again All Black tours and team selections. Pākehā awareness of Māori issues was constantly under question, by Māori from distance, but also up close by other liberal Pākehā claiming to be particularly sensitive and informed. I remember an encounter at a conference in Wellington when I was taken aside at morning tea and reprimanded by two intense young Pākehā men attending an early childhood teachers' meeting next door. They had seen me leaning on a side table with a cup of tea and wanted me to know I was being deeply offensive to Māori by leaning on a surface that might be used to serve food. It wasn't, and there were no Māori present, but it was a mark of my ignorance nonetheless. I was apologetic and embarrassed, but resented the righteous tone of their rebuke, and still do. There was a zeal and a smugness that upset me. I wondered if they had ever made the same mistake themselves, before their own moment of enlightenment. Racist as a personal accusation is a shock tactic to be used with great reluctance, and when it is, to be delivered more graciously than those kindergarten teachers managed to do to me. But I'm careful not to sit on tables anymore.

CHAPTER 7

Dreaming of rainbows

We were taking a break from the ecumenical conference we were covering in Nairobi, Kenya. There were five of us in the car, including a Kenyan reporter friend called Agnes. She had already rescued us from a customs official demanding a huge donation for breaking a regulation he invented. Now we were lost in the middle of the Amboseli National Park, in the middle of the night, in the middle of a rainstorm. Suddenly there was a shattering, metal-ripping bang and the car stopped abruptly. We sat stunned in the darkness. 'Stay still and wait,' said Agnes. 'If they don't come soon, you'll know they have gone somewhere else.' She'd been in this situation before and her confidence calmed us. It seemed this was a common occurrence. At night, bandits would erect a low wall of stones, covered with branches, across the road, then rob the motorists when they collided with it. If business was slow, the bandits would move on to richer locations, as they did in our case. The car, though damaged underneath, was eventually able to limp home and our terror subsided. But without an 'other' like Agnes, we would never have made it. I came to realise that her calmness was born out of many other encounters with violence and hardship on a scale not even remotely familiar to me.

* * *

My bicultural journey has been a stop-start affair, but the next move was more of a reframing than a stopping. Through the journalistic work I had done in Nairobi at the Assembly of the World Council of Churches (WCC), the family and I found ourselves in Geneva, Switzerland, where I worked for the WCC for 10 years, as editor and then communications director.

It was people like Agnes who continued my education in race relations. The WCC had around 300 leadership staff, many from the developing world, and in my media role I was completely dependent on their skills and insight to interpret the issues we covered. The politics of race were ever present in Geneva – quotas, racial balance and representation – and became more and more complicated as the council's membership kept growing. You had to be colour-blind to operate in that environment and my children quickly became so. When we eventually returned to New Zealand, I think that experience unconsciously influenced their choice of friends and trusted teachers. It was a Māori woman, Alva Kapa, who helped my daughter to reconnect with New Zealand, which had become a foreign country for her, and it was a Chinese Māori boy, Simon Kaan, who helped my son discover how to be a Kiwi again.

The WCC at the time was headed by the charismatic West Indian Philip Potter. His analysis of white privilege was constant and unnerving for this Pākehā New Zealander working closely alongside him as his media adviser. Western media coverage of the WCC through those years was hostile and unrelenting. Many of the council programmes were seen as dangerous – from dialogue with Islam and Buddhist faiths, support for Palestinian and other refugees, to contact with Orthodox churches behind the Iron Curtain, support for women's liberation movements and the ecumenical cause itself. But nothing compared with the furore created by the council's Programme to Combat Racism and its support for liberation movements worldwide. Grants given to groups like South Africa's African National Congress and the well-known terrorist Nelson Mandela drew the most heat but there were also grants to Indigenous groups in Australia and Māori organisations in New Zealand.

In the monthly WCC magazine, *One World*, I ran a story, based on the personal testimonies of deserters, about the Selous Scouts, which church papers like ours were the first to break. The Scouts were an elite unit of the Rhodesian forces, mostly Black soldiers, but some disguised whites, dressed as guerillas, set up to test the loyalty of villagers to the government, and where they failed, to kill or imprison them. The first-hand accounts of atrocities were horrific, deadly evidence of just how extreme and how twisted racial conflict can become. The statue of Jonathan Daniels outside the chapel at ETS in Boston kept reappearing in my mind.

The other great lesson from my WCC years was about the language required for advancing the racial justice agenda. The ecumenical movement, like other international organisations, is not good at speaking clearly so everyone can hear. That's partly because everything has to be translatable into all the official languages, using terms that make sense across cultures. Colloquialisms, humour, irony and nuance are all sacrificed for the sake of clarity. The result of all that is a bleached out jargon, a kind of 'international speak' without edge or precision, loaded with abstractions, formalities and generalities, and building a code where nothing really means what it says.

* * *

I was grateful when, in 1983, I was offered a teaching post at Knox Theological Hall in Dunedin. Jobs back home were proving hard to find: working for the WCC was no recommendation for many bishops in my own church, especially my uncle, Edward Norman, Anglican Bishop of Wellington, a respected but deeply conservative man who defended the South African government's Bantustan apartheid policies, and who deeply disapproved of my involvement in an organisation he saw as promoting terrorism. Not that we agreed on much of anything. A decade before, he had helped to ensure our failure to create a uniting church (Anglican, Congregational, Methodist and Presbyterian) in New Zealand, the cause *New Citizen* worked so hard to promote. Like so many Pākehā families, we found ourselves divided over issues of justice and racial attitudes, especially regarding the Springbok tours. Uncle Edward had been a role model for me in earlier years; now we found ourselves on opposite sides. To be so deeply at odds with someone you loved was a defining experience.

Edward was a distinguished ex-soldier, a highly decorated commander of the 25th Battalion. He was respected by Pākehā and Māori alike, though a conversation with Hone Kaa showed up the difference in the way they saw the world. Edward reprimanded Hone for being involved in blessing a traditional carving, giving spiritual significance to a lump of wood. Hone looked up at the study wall, where a picture hung of a navy frigate Edward had recently blessed in a launching ceremony. 'What were you doing there, Bishop?' he asked politely.

Back then, when denominational differences defined who you were, going to work for the Presbyterians didn't win Uncle Edward's approval. He, along with other Anglican leaders, saw it as a kind of betrayal. To me it felt entirely consistent with the ecumenical cause I'd long been working for and though I didn't realise it until I arrived in Dunedin, because about half the students in training at Knox were Pacific Islanders, mostly Samoan, I was given the chance to learn first hand about the Pasifika community. That opened up a whole new space in my cultural education.

CHAPTER 8

It's alright here

We arrived back in Auckland, bought a second-hand Ford Cortina – two-tone with walnut trim, a classy choice in 1984 – and made our way down the country, soaking up the old familiar smells and tastes. Our journey ended as we drove over the Kilmog at night and down to see the lights of Dunedin twinkling below. I knew little about the city but it felt like coming home. Not so for my two children, who hadn't lived long enough in New Zealand to remember much about it. They weren't pleased to be wrenched away from their friends and the elegance of European life. Even a Ford Cortina didn't make up for that. As they looked out from the back seat, we heard them muttering in French to each other, 'Merde, it's so small.'

* * *

Happily, my children gradually learnt to become Pākehā New Zealanders over again, though the sights and smells of Europe still excite them. For me the pull back to New Zealand was much stronger, all through our time away, for reasons that were more instinctual than rational. Our Geneva apartment was close to the airport and three times a week at 5 a.m. a plane would land direct from Singapore, with a connection on to Auckland. The sound of that flight used to wake me and I'd drift back to sleep, lulled by that aerial link with my homeland. My work colleagues in Geneva recognised that Kiwi branding in me in a bemused kind of way. The Europeans among them wore their nationalities more easily. At my farewell from the WCC they sang:

> Bluck will surely love it in New Zealand
> Sheep and kiwis and fresh air
> Yet trying to instruct a Presbyterian
> Is harder than the slopes of Val d'Isere.

Michael King wrote eloquently about this pull of home. He argued that large parts of our Pākehā identity are bound up in trace elements and memories woven into us, into our very DNA. After being away from home for nearly a decade, it all came flooding back to me in Dunedin, a city I'd only visited once before, but filled nonetheless by markers and connections that had shaped my earlier life. For instance, I felt on arrival the presence of a great-grandfather I had never met but who had lived in Dunedin, working as a ship's captain on logging boats that sailed down to the Catlins River; and a grandfather who had sung in the choir of the Anglican cathedral in the Octagon and married his Catholic beloved in the porch (not the sanctuary) of the Catholic church at Port Chalmers.

The wider cultural landscape had shifted markedly in our absence. The scars from the 1981 Springbok tour were still healing, and Merata Mita's film *Patu* about the protests was being shown in theatres, reminding everyone again of the trauma of that time. Those reminders weren't enough, however, to deter the Rugby Union from trying again to tour South Africa, until they were forced by court action to cancel in 1985, followed by the disastrous tour of the aptly named Cavaliers (as in couldn't give a stuff) the following year. The capacity of rugby to bedevil race relations continued to drive the nation apart, dishonouring its power to bring Māori and Pākehā together. The All Whites' achievement in making the finals of the football World Cup in 1982 should have been seen as a warning, even back then, that rugby's pre-eminence couldn't be taken for granted.

Muldoon was ousted from office, dragging his heels, in July 1984, and 'Poi E' hit the music charts for 22 weeks in a row, topping them for four. And the opening of the *Te Māori* exhibition in New York, that same year of our arrival home, triggered a flood of pride across the country, surprising many Pākehā with the scale and richness of the heritage it displayed to the world.

So much had changed. There was now a regular Māori language news programme on TV, a foretaste of what was to come with a fully-fledged Māori channel. The treaty was now enshrined in law and amended legislation in 1985 ensured that claims dating back to 1840 could be heard, a huge shift in scope and seriousness. The Māori Fisheries Act, four years later, though resulting in a compromise arrangement, advanced claims for customary rights much further than at any time since 1840.

These changes were not often welcomed by opinion makers in Dunedin. In 1985 Māori Affairs Minister Koro Wētere's attack on anti-Māori bias in the media drew a lecture from the *Otago Daily Times* in an editorial that makes astonishing reading now. The paper, seemingly unaware that the law had already changed to define Māori by whakapapa rather than fraction of blood quantum, accused Wētere of underrepresenting the percentage of Māori working in media because he failed to distinguish between part and full-blooded Māori. Māori complaints about the coverage they received, argued the *Otago Daily Times*, was 'not a whit different' from omissions suffered by other groups, such as highland dancers, croquet clubs and Greek Orthodox churches. The editorial concluded by asking the minister to ponder this question:

> In the media coverage of rugby, is there any suggestion
> that the media are pro-pākehā and anti-Māori? We do
> not believe it is possible for Mr Wetere to suggest there is
> any such antagonism, and the moral to be taken from this
> is that whenever Māoris simply get on with their living,
> whether by adopting pākehā or retaining Māori institutions,
> and stop worrying so much about being given special
> attention, and being treated in a special manner, they will
> get their proper share of coverage, an ample share of media
> goodwill, and a proportionate share of media shortcomings.

This was the New Zealand we came home to – or the Otago, to be precise. Pākehā identity is as regionally bound and distinctive as Māori. Both cultures have common languages but endlessly varied expressions of who they are and where they belong. Being Pākehā in Dunedin was a light year away from being Pākehā in Nūhaka, or even in Canterbury just up the road.

I began to appreciate how strange it was for Samoans brought up in Ōtara to make their way among the cold hills of Otago. But these students I taught were hugely adaptable. They found where squid, unknown to most locals, could be caught at night in the harbour basin. The patterns of student family life and study patterns became more communal, with a lot more music, shared food and laughter.

As a teacher I had to learn to adapt the way I taught my subject areas of practical theology, media and communication studies. Courses I began in New Zealand film studies proved the most popular. Pasifika students who struggled with the very formal pedagogy of much of the Bachelor of Theology university degree, flourished with the group-based participatory style of viewing and critiquing the Kiwi movies. And by the 1980s there were plenty to choose from. The drought was over and we delighted in seeing ourselves, Māori and Pākehā, on the big screen. Vincent Ward's *In Spring One Plants Alone*, *Vigil* and *Navigator*, Roger Donaldson's *Smash Palace*, Geoff Murphy's *Goodbye Pork Pie* and Billy T. James in *Came a Hot Friday* all had profound impact. It would take another 20 years for Pasifika filmmakers to be visible, but the seeds were sown in the 1980s and my students revelled in what they saw, once we found a way of engaging and learning cross-culturally.

* * *

The strongest memory of my involvement with the Pasifika community at Knox concerns the death of my father in Gisborne. I returned to Dunedin from the funeral, hoping for a quiet night to grieve alone, when there was a knock on the door. A delegation of 20 or more students and their partners waited outside, laden with baskets of food. They had come to share my sorrow. They filled our living room and an evening unfolded, very different from the one I'd planned, of singing and praying, heaps of eating and even some laughter. I couldn't have dreamt how healing that proved to be.

My father had made his own connection with this Pasifika community. When visiting he'd come with me to listen to students doing their preaching assignments in local churches on a Sunday. One of the older students, a former freezing worker from Bluff with very little formal education behind him, struggled with the academic studies and English fluency. He was a passionate preacher but sometimes hard to follow. After we listened to him perform on this Sunday morning I expressed some strong reservations to my dad, who gently disagreed. 'He's one of the most credible people I've ever listened to from a pulpit,' he told me. 'Do everything you can to let him get on with the job he's meant to be doing.'

The distinctiveness of Pākehā culture, the Dunedin variant, kept revealing itself as I dug deeper into its settler and Presbyterian roots. On Lookout Hill at the top of Signal Hill Road, above our house in Opoho, is a monument dedicated to the gritty Scottish pioneers who founded the city, armed with grim-faced Calvinism to keep the settlement pure and undefiled. Two bronze figures, male and female, hunker down, their faces turned into the southerlies that sweep up the harbour from the Antarctic. They make a stern and joyless couple. I wouldn't have known how to relate to them. And I wonder how well Māori did at the time.

One powerful way of making cross-cultural connections is walking through their physical locations. In Dunedin this took the form of pilgrimages we planned with student and ecumenical groups. One of these turned out to be the most misleading of journeys, a cautionary tale of how careful you have to be in documenting the history that makes you who you are.

There is a small but vibrant Ngāi Tahu community in Ōtepoti, Dunedin, centred on the marae at Ōtakou on the Otago Peninsula. In the 1880s their numbers were swelled by an influx of prisoners from Parihaka in Taranaki, arrested and deported for peacefully resisting the occupation of their land. The ecupilgrimage, as we cutely called it, went to Shore Street on the harbour edge, where the Parihaka prisoners were thought to have been imprisoned – 137 of them in 1879, in a cave behind a locked iron door. Inside, the roof was blackened by fire and they were supposed to have been shackled to an iron stake. It was a dramatic place to visit and to wonder how these men survived their two-year ordeal, working long days building the harbour walls.

Except it wasn't true. In 2018, after extensive and careful research by historian Seán Brosnahan, it was revealed that the prisoners were never incarcerated in the cave, and never worked on the harbour, though they did important road-building work around the city from their base in the Dunedin Gaol and were widely admired and supported by the local community. The harbourside cave remains a mystery. The most likely explanation is that it was a storage place built in the early twentieth century to keep milk cool.

Does any of that revelation lessen the impact of the Parihaka story? It was that Dunedin pilgrimage which first introduced me to that terrible day in November 1881 when Colonel John Bryce's cavalry rode through a crowd of singing children – the tātarakihi, the cicadas they were called, because of the chirping noise they made – to ransack Parihaka village. And the prisoners arrested in that invasion, though not living in a cave in Dunedin, had to put up with dreadful conditions – three died of tuberculosis – and were forced to labour in exile, as far away from their devasted home as the authorities could find.

* * *

Mainstream denominations had come very close to forming a uniting church in New Zealand in the 1970s but the Anglicans' failure to agree wrecked that effort. The 1980s brought a campaign to create a Conference of Churches in Aotearoa New Zealand (CCANZ). Largely led and driven by women, and gathering together all the mainstream churches, Protestant,

Orthodox and Catholic, the movement looked as though it would succeed, and work began with great optimism. But Māori were slow to be enthused by all this, just as they had been in the decade before. Many of them wondered how Pākehā churches, like the Anglicans, could be ready to rewrite their constitutions and lower their boundaries for the sake of ecumenical unity when they had resisted for so long any attempt to allow racial equality and equity.

Alongside the CCANZ, Māori had already formed a council of their own, Te Runanga Whakawhanaunga i nga Hahi o Aotearoa, and the Catholics had made themselves full members of this without waiting for permission from anyone. It presented the Pākehā conference with some hard challenges, especially concerning support for tino rangatiratanga, including a proposal to boycott the national elections because of a lack of progress on self-determination. The CCANZ didn't agree with the proposal; many struggled to pronounce the name, let alone meet the agenda, of Te Runanga.

The CCANZ evolved through the 1980s and came up with a strongly worded goal on bicultural partnership. But it was only one of 11 goals, not even the first on the list, and it admitted that it was open to 'misunderstanding and misrepresentation' and perhaps best described as a 'journey of learning ... by Pākehā people ... whose steps will be faltering and mistakes will be made'. Hardly a confident endorsement. Te Runanga didn't last long and with its closure came the end of any sort of liberal or progressive ecumenical alliance in Aotearoa. Conservative and fundamentalist groups took over, some modelled on the American moral majority, but the failure to find a style of ecumenical partnership that honoured both Māori and Pākehā still haunts many of us, despite half a century of trying.

My friends Hone Kaa and Rua Rakena were both leaders of Te Runanga Whakawhanaunga and they sometimes came to CCANZ meetings to monitor our progress. It felt like being observed from across a river. The gap between us was too wide even to shout across. Yet the efforts to connect continued, right to the end, not by shouting but by singing. At the meeting to finalise the constitution of the CCANZ, members of Te Runanga joined the service to celebrate the Pākehā group agreeing on a unity they had already achieved. 'We offer you our presence as you struggle to write a new song,' they said, 'a more appropriate song to sing in this land. We have our song, and we'll sing it for you.' And they did. And the silence that followed lasted for a long time.

For all its disappointments, the ecumenical movement in its various expressions had been a strong voice for treaty recognition and anti-racism education at a time when such causes were decidedly unpopular. Bob Scott, and then Mitzi Nairn, launched the national Programme on Racism effectively. Bob's biggest challenge was to focus the educational workshops on working with Pākehā alone to take responsibility for themselves and their history, rather than doing it together with Māori. Church leaders found that hard to accept; some refused, and got personal when confronting racist attitudes. The presence of well-known Māori monitors like Titewhai Harawira, invited to observe the process, often added to the heat that was generated. The Programme on Racism's focus on Pākehā self-understanding might seem obvious in retrospect, but at the time it was ground-breaking and enormously controversial, and brought a tidal shift in the bicultural debate and the evolution of Pākehā identity. To be useful treaty partners, Pākehā had to get their house in order first.

* * *

On the eve of our departure from Dunedin, Aramoana, a beautiful, empty windswept place at the mouth of Otago Harbour, became the scene of tragedy when, in mid-November 1990, David Gray shot 13 people in the seaside village. The trauma affected our family because my son and his friend Simon Kaan were surfing at Aramoana and managed to slip back through the police cordon as it closed. Simon's father Don was the greengrocer at Port Chalmers where Gray bought his tobacco and supplies each week. Don was the last person to talk to him before the shootings.

The whole event felt very close to home, and revealed the way such horror enfolds us all, regardless of our culture and place in life. Simon became a nationally known and respected artist, his work expressive of both his Chinese and Māori heritage. A huge etching by him hangs in our living room, depicting spirit figures free-falling from the hills around Aramoana, liberating themselves from the trauma that took place below.

CHAPTER 9

Cracks in the Gothic

The building of a visitors' centre alongside the Christchurch Cathedral was finally under way by 1994, after two hard years of fighting over designs and funding. The contractors were progressing well with the foundations until work suddenly had to stop: the excavation had uncovered a body. All activities were frozen as experts and inspectors, both police and regulatory, surveyed the site. They turned up evidence not of an old homicide but of a pre-European burial ground, an urupā. If the site was sacred before, it was doubly so now and further building work was impossible.

Then our Māori partners, with whom we already enjoyed a close working relationship, stepped in. Archdeacon (later Bishop) of Te Waipounamu, John Gray, assembled Ngāi Tahu elders, several of whom took time out from their jobs. Together they arranged and led a ceremony that satisfied the protocols for dealing with death, exhuming and reburying the bodies in an urupā at Tuahiwi, north of Christchurch, and allowing the cathedral's oldest witnesses to be laid to rest. Peace was restored, tapu lifted and construction resumed.

* * *

The Pākehā who established the Canterbury settlement thought they were building a miniature version of the England they still pined for. The cathedral enclosed a heritage so essentially English and Gothic that not a trace of anything Māori could be found inside it for 100 years. Yet through all that time the church was creating something on the ground of a people who had been here long before, with a spiritual and economic history of their own – fishing and trading, gardening, living and dying here, and burying their dead with great reverence.

Who was this man whose grave we stumbled into? A hunter, a warrior, a victim of Te Rauparaha's raids, a skilled practitioner of funeral rituals as the people of this area were known to be, a visitor passing through, a peaceful trader, a food gatherer in what was once a swamp? Experts speculated on all these possibilities. Whatever his role, he bore silent witness to the arrival of the first Pākehā settlers, lying there under the muddy feet of the crowd that gathered in the rain to lay the foundation stone of the cathedral in 1864, then watching the builders who erected the building, stone by stone, over 40 years. We came to know this nameless man as the 'cathedral's closest companion'.

His presence made one tiny dent in the pervasive whiteness of the cathedral and the city around it. In my 12 years there, we worked hard to make the place a little more bicultural, hugely supported by John Gray and his clergy team who helped us to establish a weekly service in te reo, and Canon Mae Taurua, a highly respected social worker and weaver, who led a project to weave large tututuku panels displayed behind the high altar. This stunning piece of traditional artwork, added to in its final stages by anyone who wanted to weave in a stitch, made a powerful contribution to easing the anxieties of those who feared we were moving too fast with what they called the 'Māori agenda'. In addition we added a Pacific Chapel, also beautifully adorned with weaving and with a carved canoe-shaped altar.

When the visitors' centre was finally completed, we planned the opening for the time Queen Elizabeth and Prince Philip visited New Zealand and invited them. The dedication in November 1995 contained some spine-tingling music with the cathedral choir of men and boys singing a classic refrain interwoven by a karanga from our kuia, weaving the two traditions together. Even the royals were impressed. 'Was that an augmented choir?' the prince asked the choirmaster in the reception line afterwards.

Occasions like that and new buildings like the visitors' centre and its story, shifted Canterbury Pākehā identity a millimetre or two in a bicultural direction, but it was always going to be hard. I knew that from the moment I arrived in Christchurch. One of my first engagements as the newly appointed dean was to speak at the venerable Canterbury Club on the banks of the Avon. Nationally known rugby and cricket commentator and vicar of Fendalton Bob Lowe was the club's honorary chaplain.

Told I could talk about what I liked, in a fit of naïvety I chose to explore Pākehā male identity. The speech didn't start until very late in the evening after copious amounts of alcohol had been consumed. I had abstained, having realised far too late that my topic might be hard for this audience of the city's great and good. And it was: the silence settled more deeply, the longer I spoke. When Bob got up to give the vote of thanks, he proceeded to shred everything I'd said into small pieces. This was a group who knew all they needed to know about Māori and the irrelevance of words like Pākehā. I went home as humiliated as I'd ever been. Years later, I asked Bob, whom I had come to know and respect for his work as a priest and a writer, whether he recalled the evening. He looked at me blankly and said he had no memory of it.

Denied or not, Pākehā identity of the Canterbury kind was formidable in its hard-edged confidence and exclusivity. I barely managed to break into its circle from the outside, despite having served my apprenticeship as a student at College House 30 years before. I seriously underestimated how tightly Pākehā Canterbury held onto its icons, particularly its rituals and buildings and furniture. So trying to make even slight changes to the annual service to celebrate the arrival of the (always capitalised) First Four Ships, such as replacing readers who were no longer able to cope, proved impossible. Every change about anything had to be negotiated with cautious, tiny steps.

Take the campaign, resisted at first, to replace the old chairs, which were long past their use-by date, with something contemporary and comfortable. It succeeded because those who donated were remembered on a plaque attached to each chair.

This wasn't simply about appealing to people's vanity: honouring generous individuals was embedded in Christchurch's culture. To be Pākehā in Canterbury, you must honour your English and settler heritage in form as well as feeling. Back in the 1990s at least, if there wasn't too much connection with Māori in shaping that identity, no one was too bothered. The rise and rise of Ngāi Tahu in visibility, influence, recognition and economic clout has changed all that. Monoculturalism is receding slowly but in the 1990s the tide was still to turn.

* * *

A measure of the bicultural temperature of Christchurch came with the 1993 cathedral service to celebrate the centenary of women's suffrage in Aotearoa. 'We remember, we claim, we pledge' was the theme of the ecumenical event. I had handed over responsibility for the planning to a group of Māori, Pākehā and Pasifika women who were far more competent than I was to create and run the event. They worked for nearly a year in preparation, involving 70 musicians, dancers, fabric artists, poets, liturgists and students from six local girls' schools. It was to be a stunning event, worked through meticulously by a process of consensus and respectful bicultural process. Prime Minister to be Jenny Shipley and Governor General Dame Cath Tizard were to attend.

And all went smoothly until the programme for the service was pre-released. A very angry official from the Ministry of Internal Affairs called to berate me for not taking control of my cathedral: how dare I allow such a service to proceed. The offending part of the service proved to be a liturgical danced confession by Pākehā women acknowledging their part in 'the acceptance of violent and unjust relationships between the tangata whenua and tauiwi' and admitting that, by their silence and collusion with those in power, they had condoned injustice, that they had enjoyed privileges denied their Māori sisters, that they had claimed what was not rightfully theirs and 'been party to the repression of the culture and tradition of the Māori, whose land Aotearoa is'. In 'claiming a national identity' they had 'failed to claim the treaty' and had supported education, health and justice systems that did not reflect 'a just Māori–tauiwi relationship'. The women wore grey shrouds, which were then removed during words of commitment and forgiveness.

This was hard, prophetic stuff, too hard for the Ministry of Internal Affairs when I refused to intervene or try to change anything. The service proceeded. Jenny Shipley did attend. Cath Tizard did not, citing 'concerns about a part of the service which had not been resolved'. Opposition leader Mike Moore said the whole thing was 'Star Chamber tactics. We don't hold the present generation of Germans answerable for the war and we should not be imprisoned by history, rather we should learn from it.'

A deluge of mail followed, almost all from offended women, including members of the Canterbury Federation of University Women. 'There is no logic in calling for women to repent for 100 years of dominance of Māori women,' wrote one, 'when most of us in the 30s and 40s did not have the opportunity to meet Māoris because of their low population numbers in this area.' That was a common refrain from Pākehā Canterbury: We don't know any Māori so how can we be sorry for what's happened? 'I do not condone injustice and never have,' wrote a prominent Christchurch woman. 'I consider myself as much a New Zealander as anyone else whose forebears came to this country. They may have arrived later than the Māoris, but they still came from across the sea and probably for the same reasons. For people such as you to try to place a burden of guilt on us because our ancestors came later than the Māoris, is I believe, a most unchristian action.'

Pākehā resentment at Māori protest and complaint grew rapidly through the 1990s as legal reforms, land claim settlements and treaty recognition accelerated, especially following its 150th anniversary at Waitangi, attended by Queen Elizabeth. Archbishop Whakahuihui Vercoe used the occasion to remind her of the Crown's failure to honour the treaty her great-grandmother had made with Māori. The National government's attempts to impose a 'fiscal envelope' ceiling on treaty settlements didn't last and big gains had been made by the end of the decade, especially for Ngāi Tahu and Tainui.

Media talked of a 'grievance industry', which spawned a form of art to express it. I wrote a book in this period called *Killing Me Softly: Challenging the Kiwi Culture of Complaint*.

That culture was deep seated, and still is, and spread well beyond any racial agenda. But it did help to shape the bicultural debate at the time. As Tā Tipene O'Regan of Ngāi Tahu said at the time, 'It's the grievance itself that gives some people their identity.' He might have added, 'just as it does for those who take offence at the grievance.'

John Coley, former director of Christchurch's McDougall Art Gallery who interpreted many New Zealand artists, both Māori and Pākehā, with sympathy and respect, had this to say about the Kiwi school of 'grievance art', which he described in a December 2000 *Press* article as 'the art of racial disharmony, of blame, shame and victimhood, overlord and underdog, of long resented wrongs and carefully maintained anger. Grievance art calls racism for what it is, shakes its fist, or weeps with the martyr's despair in the face of middle class anxiety. Its painted polemics pick at the scabs of our bicultural history, keep the hurt needled, and don't allow the old wounds to heal.' He probably had two particular artists in mind, both of them exhibiting at the Venice Biennale: Jacqueline Fraser, well known for her allegories of colonial destruction, and Peter Robinson, notorious at the time for his swastika with the attached legend, 'Pākehā have rights too.'

Coley argued that our national identity shouldn't be shown, especially overseas, as 'riven by racial discord when great progress has been made to settle the grievances of the past … and New Zealand's culture is more complex, more sophisticated, more tolerant of difference, and willing to change than some social critics give us credit for.' This argument – that we shouldn't be washing the dirty linen of our colonial past too often or too publicly, that labouring over what's wrong stops us from moving on – was familiar and common among Pākehā in the 1990s, especially in Canterbury, and it persists today.

* * *

Giving so-called grievance art a whole new twist were some TV and film productions that reshaped the bicultural debate. *Once Were Warriors* hit the screen in 1994, drawing huge Pākehā audiences while also serving to escalate Māori stereotyping. Some commentators argued the film reinforced the idea that Māori were innately different to Pākehā, subject to poverty and violence in a way that Pākehā were not, saddled with a warrior legacy that was somehow genetic. In their view, this widened the distance between the cultures, making it easier to blame the victim for these problems. Māori would have to help themselves and there was nothing that Pākehā could do about it, even as they watched the violence on screen with fascinated horror. For Pākehā who had little personal contact with Māori, this didn't help to change attitudes.

A more positive experience awaited in James Belich's five-part 1998 TV series on the New Zealand Wars. Many Pākehā discovered for the first time just what a sophisticated and effective fighting force Māori were, especially with guerilla-style Viet Cong strategies, and trench warfare systems not seen again until the First World War. Belich detailed just how often the British forces were humiliated by a less armed and equipped foe and how narrowly they avoided defeat. Once again, stereotypes tumbled.

I used my media platforms, as a *Press* columnist and a Radio New Zealand broadcaster, as well as the cathedral pulpit, to try to interpret this changing bicultural landscape. And it *was* changing, both in Canterbury and nationally, helped by my own church adopting a revolutionary new constitution that gave equal voice to three tikanga – Māori, Pākehā and Pasifika – ending a 140-year halt on Māori self-determination. A church that had started so proudly as Te Hāhi Mihinare, a Māori-led missionary church, had become a settler-dominated church that did not consider Māori ready for leadership. All that ended with the constitutional reform of 1992.

It was followed up by a call in 1998 for a general strike to protest the growing levels of poverty and inequality, but this morphed into a Hikoi of Hope, starting from both the north and south of the country. When the southern marchers reached Christchurch, we hosted them in the square in front of the cathedral. There was a strong Māori presence, both among the marchers, who had begun their journey in Bluff, and through the local Ngāi Tahu leaders gathered to welcome them. The whole occasion was shaped by tangata whenua. I was a bit taken aback to receive complaints from usually liberal church congregations wishing that the speeches had been shorter and hadn't used so much Māori language. The two ends of the hikoi converged in Wellington with a crowd of 5000 in Parliament grounds calling for economic and, even more controversially, constitutional reform, not just for the church, but the whole country. Prime Minister Shipley was not impressed.

I also kept returning, in my columns and broadcasts, to the way the media, by their coverage, often predetermined the outcome of bicultural issues. The Christchurch Polytechnic's nursing school controversy in 1993 was a case in point. Irihapeti Ramsden had done pioneering work in cultural safety programmes for both Māori and Pākehā nurses, to help them work sensitively and effectively with Māori patients. The Christchurch school had put this pioneering work into practice, but not with the approval of one young Pākehā student who claimed she'd been 'bounced out' of a course for arguing with a kaumātua over not being allowed to speak on the marae and alleging that a tutor had told her Māori printing presses were thrown into the sea by Pākehā.

What should have been treated as an internal squabble became a national story overnight. The media pounced on the student's complaints, then only very belatedly sought a considered Māori response. 'The whole affair,' I wrote at the time, 'showed an incredible ignorance of Māori spirituality, a total disregard of Treaty obligations in educational delivery and a deep anxiety about Christchurch's ability to develop a bicultural identity.' The incident would have disappointed a refugee from Auckland who had been quoted in the *Press* that same week as saying that he and his family had come down to Christchurch to get away from 'ethnic troubles up north'.

When the government and the Māori Fisheries Commission signed up to buy Sealord's fishing interest for Māori, coverage focused on whether Māori would ever be able to agree among themselves for long enough to cement the deal. TV current affairs programmes went looking for Māori dissenters and revelled in any disunity they found. There was never a reference to the massively greater Pākehā disunity over the issue. The assumption was that Pākehā people, unlike Māori, were all so different that they couldn't be expected to agree on much of anything, but Māori should. My broadcast on the subject argued that the fishing deal was being made as part of a treaty settlement, the same treaty that gave Pākehā the moral, legal and spiritual right to be here, but they hadn't yet learnt how to discover and enjoy the confidence that comes from having a culture of their own – not one imported from London, or one borrowed from Māori.

The other criticism of media I kept repeating in these years was its habit of covering very different stories but always with the same focus on conflict. A 1995 *Morning Comment* broadcast compared two stories that received exactly the same style of coverage: the campaign to assemble a new Australasian structure for rugby league competition, and the occupation of Moutoa Gardens and the Pākaitore pā site in Whanganui that had been going on for seven weeks. It may as well have been the seventh minute, for all the insight the media coverage brought, singling out the most anxious people on both sides, fastening on any deadline that put everyone involved under pressure, focusing only on the present moment and ignoring the history behind it all, collecting the most inflammatory remarks and endlessly replaying every hint of violence. Completely overlooked was the complexity of Pākaitore's history as a fishing settlement and trading centre, a military base and parade ground, land that had been fought over and hallowed and designated and confiscated and renegotiated until the very stones cried out.

Shortly after this, I made a pilgrimage of my own to Pākaitore. By then the occupation was over. It had become a quiet place again, though there was still evidence to show the aftermath of the bitter confrontations. The pond where a child had drowned during the protest had been filled in. Empty pedestals marked where offending statues had been removed, and words had been defaced on an inscription honouring 'the defence of law and order against fanaticism and barbarism'. On the autumn morning when I walked through, the only sign of life was two teenage girls, one Pākehā, one Māori, chatting happily, unbothered by the weight of history around them that had shaped them both.

* * *

That pilgrimage was one of many I made through those Christchurch years, providing me with perhaps the most powerful lesson in my bicultural education. After a decade of being immersed in city affairs, these journeys were driven by wanting to find the pulse of the country again through hitting the road and trusting it to show me something new. Increasingly, I felt the most important things about being a New Zealander were still lying around on the edges of Kiwi culture. Important things, like flair and innovation, nerve, imagination, the ability to laugh easily, knowing how to live happily with less, and the confidence to feel comfortable as you are, in your own skin. Finding just where these little places were meant making journeys outside Canterbury. Maybe I would find towns higher above sea level that were less cantankerous. I wanted to break out of the plastic wrap of familiar territory for a while, so, with Liz, I hit the road. The places we visited then, nearly 30 years ago, stay with me and shape my sense of who I am as Pākehā; a sense that comes often by contrast as much as companionship with Māori.

At Parihaka, under the shadow of the mountain, we stood at the place where hundreds of children from the village, laughing and singing, went out to meet Colonel John Bryce's troops, ordered to destroy the settlement as punishment for the passive resistance campaign led by Tohu and Te Whiti, a campaign known and honoured worldwide, which took the form of ploughing up the surveyors' pegs that marked out the encroachment of the settler farmers. In Featherston in Wairarapa, we stood on the site of the camp, New Zealand's largest, which trained some 60,000 young men, my uncles among them, to fight in the First World War. Many of the 16,000 who never returned began their short-lived military careers here. It was a place for 'hardening up', as the marble plaque says, before the route march over the Rimutaka Range and the boarding of troopships in Wellington.

And as if to remind us that in every hard place in the Pākehā story there is a dark corner, the Featherston camp site also holds the story of the 800 Japanese prisoners of war who were held here during the Second World War, and the 48 who were killed, along with one guard, and the 63 wounded when they resisted their confinement, one nightmare day in February 1943. People still struggle to talk about what happened there, despite a play, a book and a TV programme or two airing the story. The Japanese government has marked the site with a row of cherry trees and a lone inscription on a concrete seat that reads, 'Behold the summer grass. All that remains of the dreams of warriors.'

When I asked a local why there wasn't more information at the site about what happened, he paused and replied, 'I think there will be one day. But it will take another generation yet.' Pākehā speaking is like that – often terse, laconic, holding back too much emotion. Showing your feelings too openly, wearing your heart on your sleeve, especially about the bad stuff, is still frowned upon. That's what our fathers taught us when they came home from war and sat in silence, smoking, drinking, wondering why they couldn't ever reclaim what they had known before.

Our pilgrimage took us all over the North Island, all the way up to Cape Reinga/Te Rerenga Wairua, where we felt the spirits' presence. You needed to be careful where you trod up there as a Pākehā pilgrim. The Department of Conservation signs reminded you, 'This is spiritual and sacred land. Please do not consume food and drink', and then at the end of the walkway, in case you'd forgotten who you were, 'Please no access beyond this point for ecological and cultural reasons.'

Those reminders were everywhere in the Far North. At the Bluff Beach well up Te-Oneroa-a-Tōhē/Ninety Mile Beach, described on the maps as 'best fishing' – an invitation I'd die to try – a sand-blasted sign said access to the rocks is at the sole discretion of the tribal trustees. No contact details provided. And further down the west coast, around the Kaipara Harbour, there were fragments, but only fragments, mostly housed in the Kauri Museum at Matakohe, of a vast kauri forest that Pākehā felled to build houses for Auckland and ships for the British Navy. No wonder the bicultural relationships can be tense up here. It's a mixed story on the Pākehā side, perhaps even more so than for Māori, despite the stereotype that Ngāpuhi can never agree on anything, let alone a treaty settlement.

That North Island search for Pākehā identity spurred me to do the same in the south, and back in Christchurch we at the cathedral began a programme of bus journeys around the island, visiting places that forged what it meant to be Pākehā on the Mainland. Our partnership with Te Wai Pounamu Anglicans, led by John Gray and Mae Taurua and their Ngāi Tahu cousins, and the access they ensured, was crucial for this venture.

The power of these journeys was clear from one of the earliest trips: a short ride out beyond Rangiora to the site of the original Te Wai Pounamu Māori Girls' College, opened in 1909. The original house was now a private residence, beautifully redecorated and set in a lovely garden. The new owners kindly allowed us to visit and looked on curiously as the story they had never heard of the original school was told, based on first-hand accounts from former pupils. It was a story of rare opportunity for Māori in the early twentieth century, but also a story of hardship and deprivation. Funding was precarious, support from the Pākehā church frugal at best; staff had to make do with whatever resources they could scrape together. One account described the girls learning to sew underwear made from recycled flour bags and feeling the shame of that. The owners, listening in from a corner of the garden, wept quietly as they heard what had happened in their house.

Other pilgrimages went much further afield. To Banks Peninsula, Horomaka, and up to Kaiapoi to follow the destructive trail of Ngāti Toa chief Te Rauparaha, and then the peacemaking mission of his son Tamihana, who followed him. Then over to the West Coast, Te Tai Poutini, and the Arahura River, following the trails of the greenstone hunters and learning to identify the beautiful pounamu in the riverbed and understand its spiritual importance. Then down to the Mackenzie Country to Omarama, led by a Waitaha elder to the ancient cave drawings, the country's oldest art gallery, and following the steps of the prophet Hipa Te Maihāroa, who led his people on another pilgrimage, this one of protest over the unscrupulous and massive removal of their land. It was a story that ended in armed intervention in 1879 by the Ōamaru Constabulary, under orders to 'deal with the Māoris at Omarama in the same fashion as Te Whiti's ploughmen had been dealt with at Parihaka'. Few Canterbury Pākehā had ever heard of this epic story, as dramatic as anything up north, although it was widely reported in the press at the time in the most lurid prose, all to do with a magical figure, bizarre and exotic enough to be quickly forgotten. Our pilgrimage helped to shift that caricature, as did, rather more significantly, Buddy Mikaere's book on Te Maihāroa, which we celebrated in the cathedral.

* * *

My time in Christchurch was coming to a close. Living and working in the city centre, I'd encountered a few 'other' figures. Two stand out. When the Twin Towers fell in 2001, we held a service in the cathedral to help people deal with the shock. Hundreds poured in and as I led the event from the front, I could see a small group of black-clad and veiled women slip in and quietly tuck themselves away into the back of the crowd. I found later they were from the local Muslim community. To come and join the mourning, dressed in their hijabs, must have taken great courage. It was long before the Christchurch mosque massacre, and the Muslim community was still a barely visible force in the city. The silent presence of these women challenged me profoundly.

As did a young man I'll call Fred, who knocked on the back door of the cathedral one day, asking to see a priest. He was a member of one of the city's notorious White Power gangs and was trying to get out. The price of leaving was several hundred dollars more than what he could scrounge together. He told me awful stories of the violence in which he'd been complicit and to which he was now subject, and I believed him. I lent him money. He returned several times to ask for more, as the cost of departure kept rising, until I had to refuse any more help. Weeks went by, until there was another knock on the back door and

Fred returned to tell me what had happened. His mouth was a dreadful mess. The gang bosses had smashed his teeth with a hammer and thrown him out. He needed to get out of town and wanted my help. I paid for his bus ticket and never saw or heard from him again. For me, he became an 'other' like no other, his life a soakpit of racist rants, desperation and despair.

Like all the 'others' I've met, the Muslim women and the lost young man refused to fit neatly into ethnic categories. Auckland University academic Elizabeth Rata argues that the Māori–Pākehā debate has become captive to what she calls 'ethno nationalism', whereby a person's most essential self is defined by race rather than humanity. That hasn't been my experience. The Māori leaders I've encountered have all been men and women whose grace and generosity overflow any sort of racial containment. And the 'others' I have known have the same effect of dissolving and overriding ethnic boundaries and removing defining labels.

CHAPTER 10

Finding the thin places

He knocked on the back door of the cathedral one morning, a Māori priest from Hawke's Bay I hadn't seen for years. He stood on the steps, refusing to come inside. 'I just need to say to you,' he said, 'it's time you came home.' He walked off into the square and I never got to see him again because he died soon afterwards.

* * *

The interview that led to my election as the Anglican Bishop of Waiapu took place at an address I knew well in Napier. At one end of the street was the army drill hall where my uncle had first tried to enlist in 1939, lying about his age. His mother, my grandmother, put on her hat and went down to set the record straight, thus delaying his military career. I used to visit Grandma on Friday afternoons in the 1950s, at the other end of the same street, as a hungry and homesick boarder, to stock up on biscuits.

The Waiapu years were the most intense in my bicultural education. I travelled across the three different regions of the

huge diocese, from Woodville in Hawke's Bay in the south up
to Tauranga and Rotorua in the Bay of Plenty and across to
the East Coast. Each region was distinct in its culture, giving
different shape to what it meant to be Pākehā. In Art Deco-ed
Napier, apart from Pania sitting on her reef as a bronzed beauty
on Marine Parade, evidence of the Māori partner was hard to
find. In Gisborne the evidence was everywhere, with even the
symbols of James Cook's visit being renegotiated.

The bicultural agenda was always central in Waiapu. The
Māori presence had defined the diocese from the beginning.
In the 1880s its governing synod was conducted in te reo and
until the new constitution separated Anglicans into tikanga
in 1992, Māori were always visibly dominant. I saw my job as
strengthening that partnership through funding for unpaid
clergy on the East Coast, introducing more te reo into liturgies,
promoting shared events, renegotiating and making the shared
story more accessible through publications, historical research,
shared education programmes and, most importantly, through
a year of pilgrimage. My Pākehā colleague, Bishop George
Connor, a fluent te reo speaker, made a huge contribution to all
of this.

This new stage in my journey was a mixture of comfort
and acute discomfort. Comfort because I was coming home to
familiar places and faces, and roads, especially roads, where I
spent most of my time behind a steering wheel. I drove the same
highways my father had as a truck driver in the 1920s and 1930s,
when he hauled wool bales to Napier port and caught an hour

or two's sleep on the way home, always at the same spot on the road, slung in a hammock under the truck deck. Our family called that place Willow Creek Motel. There were lots of places like that on my journeys. They served to anchor me into the landscape, each little Pākehā piece of it.

This business of building an identity is only done piece by piece, fragment on top of fragment. Like the bits of broken crockery scattered across the paddocks at Waerenga-a-Hika outside Gisborne. In 1857 Bishop William Williams had established training schools for ordinands and other church workers there, along with his residence and the diocesan headquarters. The property was destroyed in November 1865 when the 800 Pai Mārire sympathisers in the nearby pā were attacked and defeated by a combined Ngāti Porou and Pākehā force. Founded by Te Ua Haumene in 1862, Pai Mārire (meaning good and peaceful and also known as Hau Hau) was a religious movement prophetic and charismatic in character, which drew on both traditional Māori and European Christian elements. It strongly influenced later Māori leaders, including Te Whiti and Tohu and Tītokowaru. To the European population the movement was much derided as a violent and fanatical sect. More than a century and a half after the battle, fragments of china resurface every year during spring ploughing, reminders of a shared story that will not let itself be forgotten. As witness to the fact that we *did* remember, we commissioned a tall carving that still overlooks the site of the school and honours all that it achieved, in spite of its destruction.

Familiar places, and faces, my father's included. Although he had died several years before, he was still remembered. 'You're Edgar's boy' was a better entry ticket than wearing a purple shirt. And Norman Lesser, the bishop who ordained me, was still a legendary figure in Waiapu: he had arrived as bishop from Liverpool via Kenya and stayed for a lifetime. Short in stature, a great storyteller, he was welcomed by Māori with a speech that described how they went fishing for him overseas and 'landed a shrimp'. Ever the English bishop in frock coat and gaiters, he worked tirelessly, despite the constraints of the Pākehā culture of the 1950s, to promote forums like the Hui Topu, which gathered Māori Anglicans in celebration of their culture, language and faith. He had supported me through all my wanderings and my loyalty to him had helped to bring me home. And Paul Reeves, his successor, whose advocacy for the Clergy for Rowling campaign had drawn the fury of Hawke's Bay farmer National Party voters, some of whom came to warn me against such political temptations when I arrived to follow him. And my old housemaster, Alan Howlett, musician, librarian, teacher and embroiderer, the man who introduced Saturday night movies in Cinemascope and Technicolor to Napier Boys' High, brightening the spartan life of a boarder.

Loyalties to these people and a hundred more made up the tapestry of who I was, a kind of whakapapa decades deep. One day that will be centuries deep, as it is for Māori, but it was still deep enough to define me. These were the trace elements of who I was as Pākehā, feeding a chemistry of memory and place, experiences and imaginings.

And there were some remarkable new colleagues. Leo Te Kira, for instance, a Māori priest appointed as vicar of Waipukurau. Some of the parishioners wondered about the appointment, not because he was Māori, but because he lived with cerebral palsy and couldn't drive, which some saw as a cardinal sin for a country vicar.

'How would you ever be able to come and visit me?' asked one leading parishioner. 'I live four kilometres out of town. What if I invited you to come and have breakfast with me?'

'What time would you like me to come?' Leo replied.

Taken aback, she replied, 'About nine o'clock.'

Leo paused for a moment, then replied, 'Well, I'd set off walking at 6.30 and be there in plenty of time.'

The woman became one of Leo's strongest supporters and helped to organise a roster of volunteer drivers to assist his ministry in this parish, which was rich in Pākehā folklore. The bell ringer was famous for prolonging the peals before the service to cover the arrival of his mother, who sang in the choir and was notorious for being late.

Another key Māori colleague with a skilled and intuitive ability to work biculturally was Jack Papuni of Ngāti Porou, who became a key member of my leadership team. It was through his mana that we were able to access many marae, during our year of pilgrimage, which would have been closed to us. These were the sort of partnerships that turned the search for Pākehā identity from a hard ride into an exhilarating one.

But there was an uncomfortable side to all this as well. The fear and trembling you felt when having to stand and respond to a marae welcome, with a memorised speech you could only stumble through, responding to things said about you that you only slightly understood, and with no subtlety or humour. And the shame from witnessing humiliations and slights for Māori colleagues, some of which you were unintentionally party to, some of which you inherited responsibility for.

In 1907 the Waiapu Synod had condemned the actions of the Tūhoe prophet Rua Kēnana Hepetipa, thereby ensuring that Anglicans would not be welcome again in Te Urewera. As a result of a pilgrimage we made to the site of Rua's Maungapōhatu community 100 years later, we were able to achieve some reconciliation and issue a formal apology for that earlier condemnation. I was less successful in achieving an apology with my other bishops for the judgement they had once passed on another prophet, Tahupōtiki Wiremu Rātana, who was excommunicated back in 1928. We still have a lot of history to set right.

* * *

For many of the pilgrims who took part in our year of journeys, being Pākehā was not an identity they'd thought much about, living as they did in communities where Māori had not recently asserted their presence or reminded anyone about their historic partnership. Many found it challenging and sometimes confronting to find that the now mostly Pākehā church they thought they understood had a history that was long defined and driven by Māori energy and vision.

At Rangitukia we heard how William Williams, when he first arrived there in the 1830s, found the locals were already familiar with the prayer book service and hymns he led, even to the point of correcting his choice of tunes. The same happened on his first visit to Napier in 1840 when 100 people assembled for his first service. This was all due to the work of Māori catechists and teachers who had trained at the mission station at Paihia 15 years before and brought the Bible and its message home to their people. Even from the beginning, evangelism had been an enterprise led and shaped by Māori, not at all reliant on Pākehā initiative.

That sort of bicultural interdependence was evident everywhere we went, sometimes remembered happily, sometimes not. In Ōpōtiki we heard from kaumātua Te Riaki Amoamo about the devastation created for his Whakatōhea people when 490,000 acres, almost 200,000 hectares, were confiscated in retaliation for the killing of the missionary Carl Völkner. The falsely directed charge drew an apology from the government a century later, but the land and restoration issues remain unresolved. We heard that story and also listened to the families of Pākehā settlers who had benefited with land from those confiscations. We gathered over a roast dinner in the Ōpōtiki Club, surrounded by deer antlers on the walls, alongside the snooker tables. We fit into this community as 'comfortably as an old shoe' said one farmer, who didn't lie awake at night worrying about his Pākehā identity.

But there was often a chasm between two versions of the same story, which still opened a vein of unease about being Pākehā. In Tauranga we visited the Elms mission station where, at the end of April 1864, on the eve of the Battle at Gate Pā, Pukehinahina, Archdeacon Alfred Brown entertained the British officers with a dinner party and offered them communion afterwards. The dinner table and its setting were preserved in the dining room. The names of the guests are known because they can all be found on gravestones nearby: all but one of them were killed the next day in the fighting. No one knows the names of the Māori who watched the meal through the window. They were all Brown's friends and students, baffled and betrayed by their exclusion from the occasion.

Those chasms of understanding in the same shared history are further complicated by the fact that many Māori fought other Māori on the side of British troops and Pākehā militia in the New Zealand Wars. They were called Kūpapa or Queenites, and many came from Ngāti Porou and Ngāti Kahungungu. Though some labelled them traitors, the reality was more complex. More often they were fighting under the promise of government protection and for the longer term interests of their iwi, where their first loyalty lay. Traditional tribal enemies could be a bigger threat than Pākehā. The stories of these kūpapa are found all across Waiapu. The Anglican missionary Rēnata Kawepō trained at Paihia and was travelling companion to Bishop George Selwyn and to William Colenso, the missionary who printed the Treaty of Waitangi and witnessed its signing. He fought Te Kooti in Te

Urewera and later the Pai Mārire forces at Ōmarunui outside Napier in the infamous One Day War of 1866. As Hawke's Bay's leading chief, Kawepō established sheep farms and flour mills across the region, built roads and bridges and supported numerous schools, including Te Aute College.

The prophet Te Kooti Arikirangi Te Turuki's story is equally entwined with Pākehā. He was much distorted in earlier histories, but Judith Binney's ground-breaking *Redemption Songs* showed him as a visionary leader.

Te Kooti was a friend and student of the missionary Thomas Grace, who encouraged him to train as an Anglican priest, but he fell out with the mission and became caught up in the fighting with government forces against Pai Mārire at Waerenga-a-Hika, was wrongfully accused as a spy, imprisoned and exiled to Chatham Island (Wharekauri). His visionary experiences there led to him founding the Ringatū faith and finding his role as a prophet and healer. He escaped from Wharekauri and with his forces returned to the Gisborne area, seeking unsuccessfully to be allowed to move peacefully up to the Waikato. Hostilities began again locally as he led raids in revenge for his earlier betrayal, inflicting more deaths on the local Rongowhakaata people than on Pākehā. He fled to the mountains of Te Urewera, where Pākehā militia and kūpapa troops pursued him for nearly a decade.

When our pilgrimage left Gisborne to trace Te Kooti's flight through Te Urewera, Rongowhakaata elder Stan Pardoe gave us his blessing and asked us to pray for his own people who were forced to go with Te Kooti and died in the mountains. The whakarau, the bound ones, he called them. Bicultural partnership doesn't get much more complicated than that.

Although perhaps it does. Te Kooti was eventually pardoned and devoted the last 20 years of his life as a spiritual leader to peaceful and lawful causes, following many deadly encounters across the region, including an attack on Armed Constabulary outside Taupō at Opepe, in which nine men died. The two sons of Te Kooti's mentor and friend, Thomas Grace, farmed there. When they met Te Kooti much later, they told the old warrior that he had nearly killed them that day. 'If I'd known that you were the sons of Mr Grace,' he replied, 'no harm would have come to you.'

Cultural entanglement can be overwhelming in its complexity. Outside the door of St Faith's Church at Ōhinemutu on the shore of Lake Rotorua, highly regarded in the Māori world, is the gravestone of Captain Gilbert Mair, who in 1869 led cavalry columns of Te Arawa soldiers in the hunt for Te Kooti. The battle flags of those campaigns hang above the door of the church, laid up in 1924 with the words, 'To fight in an honourable cause is more truly Christian than cowardice.' Little wonder, then, that a bust of Queen Victoria on the marae across the road from the church has disappeared on several occasions.

In the late 1840s William Colenso, missionary, preacher, peacemaker, botanist, explorer and politician, who was married with two children, had an affair with a young housemaid called Rīpeka, who bore him a son named Wiremu. After his wife

Elizabeth found out, she sent her son and daughter to family in Auckland and followed them a year later, with Wiremu. The boy was returned to his father's care in 1861. Elizabeth became a teacher, and later a sought-after translator. Colenso was dismissed from mission work for his infidelity and spent many years working in politics, botany and writing. Near the end of his very long life, he was readmitted to the Anglican clergy and appointed to serve the church in Woodville. On one of our pilgrimages there we dedicated a plaque in his memory and told the story of his son. In the middle of the service a man stepped out of congregation, a funeral director from Manawatu, and announced that he was Wiremu's great-great-grandson. So it goes.

There weren't many children involved in the journeys, but nine-year-old Emma Macguire went on two and wrote about them afterwards. Her memories grounded the whole exercise, not in the abstractions of identity seeking, but in the down-to-earth stuff of the ordinary and the everyday. 'Best part of all was climbing trees, like the ones outside St Andrew's Church in Tolaga Bay … At Rangitukia we stayed two nights on the marae. It was the first time I slept in a meeting house. It was fun. I liked the food a lot, it was yummy. Some people complained about the snoring, but it didn't bother me.' She described having morning tea at Gate Pa 'and then went to the cemetery where there were soldiers' graves'. Later, at Te Ranga, Emma wrote that she 'picked daisies in the long grass and played with a ball. It was hard to imagine a battle had taken place in that field.

It started to rain so we got into the cars quickly and went for afternoon tea.'

* * *

Through the Waiapu years I continued to broadcast and write, including a column for the *Dominion Post*. There were plenty of standout bicultural milestones to comment on, such as the return of the Unknown Warrior in 2004. Of the 30,000 New Zealand soldiers who have died in overseas wars, a third lie in unknown graves. In order to remember all of them, the decision was made to bring home the remains of just one soldier from a foreign field. The idea had been around since 1921, when the government declined to follow the British example in Westminster Abbey. Over 80 years later, the remains of a nameless young Kiwi were disinterred from a grave on the Western Front, near Longueval in France, under a headstone that simply read, 'A New Zealand soldier of the Great War known to God'. We'll never know whether he was from Khandallah or Kaikohe, whether he was one of those who marched over the Rimutaka Hill from Featherston Camp, whether he was Pākehā, or a Māori from the New Zealand Pioneer Battalion sent to dig trenches. Whoever he was, he lies now at the National War Memorial in Wellington, in a kauri casket carved by a brother soldier, in a tomb of black granite, inlaid with crosses of Tākaka marble, which signify those left behind in overseas graves and the stars in the sky. The Tomb of the Unknown Warrior, Te Toma o te Toa Matangaro, is topped by a bronze mantle, embossed with pounamu. And around the base of the tomb, in Māori and English, are the words of the karanga, which begins: 'Te mamae nei a te pōuri nui/ Tēnei ra e te tau' – The great pain we feel/Is for you who were our future. It is difficult to think of a better symbol of the losses that haunt and bind us as two cultures embroiled in shared wars.

Also etched into hearts throughout Aotearoa was a very different internment a couple of years before, when the remains of the country's first Catholic bishop, Jean Baptiste Pompallier, were brought back from France to be buried again under the altar of St Mary's, Motuti, overlooking the Hokianga Harbour. Pompallier had been present at Waitangi for the signing of the treaty, which he viewed with suspicion for its failure to guarantee freedom of religion, but respect among Māori and Pākehā alike for his pioneering mission has only grown over the years. Before he reached Motuti, Pompallier, in a glass-topped casket, made a three-month national tour of Catholic churches, great and small. Wairoa was one of the small ones, too small in fact – the doorway wasn't wide enough to accommodate the casket. But quick thinking and a dash of Kiwi ingenuity produced an instant fix in the form of a chainsaw that soon widened the door frame. Problem solved.

The tangihanga of Māori Queen Te Arikinui Dame Te Atairangikaahu, in 2006, was another hallmark of the bicultural calendar in those years. Derek Fox headed a commentary team providing joint Māori Television/TVNZ broadcast of the funeral, which was watched by 430,000 people. The journey of the waka escorting her body up the Waikato River from

Tūrangawaewae to her burial on Mount Taupiri made engrossing viewing, especially for those Pākehā who were being introduced to the depth and richness of the tikanga governing death and mourning. It was in the shadow of that same mountain, a decade before, that Doug Graham had pulled over onto the roadside, suddenly overwhelmed and in tears, realising what was at stake for Aotearoa's future in achieving the treaty settlements for which he, as minister, was responsible.

The Hikoi of Hope in 1998 had drawn 5000 people to the grounds of Parliament. The march to the same destination in 2004, protesting against the government's proposed foreshore and seabed legislation, drew 15,000. That controversy, which gave birth to the Māori Party/Te Pāti Māori and produced an Act that was repealed six years later, put the coastline into public ownership. It granted Māori some limited claims to guardianship and customary rights but failed to satisfy either side. This remains a divisive issue in the bicultural partnership.

Equally contentious, though they ended in official apologies, were the 2007 raids on Ruatoki aimed at supposed paramilitary units being trained by Tūhoe in Te Urewera. Seventeen people were arrested, and 291 charges laid under the Arms Act, but only four convictions eventuated, none of them under the Suppression of Terrorism legislation. It was a massive setback for bicultural progress and sent the police into damage-control mode. It also made for lurid media coverage.

By then I was nearing retirement age and the end of my season in Waiapu. I had no influence over the choice of my successor as bishop but there was at least a good chance of a Māori candidate being chosen, a reasonable hope that the bicultural funding and pilgrimages would continue, and I might remain involved. It didn't work out as I'd hoped and we ended up in a very different bicultural landscape.

CHAPTER 11

Becoming a retiring Pākehā

The opening graphics of the TV series *The Good Fight* show a series of familiar objects – phones, handbags, computers, flower vases – being blown to smithereens. They would make a great introduction to my retirement story, which began with moving to Pakiri, a quiet and tiny coastal village about an hour and a half from gridlocked Auckland. With a strong Māori community, Pakiri seemed like a good place to reflect on a lifelong bicultural journey. Trouble was, so much of what had happened on that journey seemed to be exploding. In Christchurch, the cathedral and its visitors' centre fell over in the 2011 earthquake and in 2019 the peaceful city itself, and the nation, was traumatised by a massacre. The college where I'd taught in Dunedin was downsized unrecognisably, the ecumenical programmes and other initiatives I'd worked for closed down. The World Council of Churches had shrunk in less than a decade to a shadow of its former size and influence. My old friend Hone died not long after I moved to Pakiri, and contact with the Māori colleagues I'd worked with faded away. All these things happened, if not suddenly, then certainly with unnerving haste. The bicultural relationships that had framed so much of my life began to seem elusive and, for all its progress, the wider, national partnership seemed more often to falter and descend into stand-off and distance.

* * *

Pakiri is not all that far north of Auckland, but it might as well be on the other side of the moon, for all that the Super City knows or cares. And when it does take an interest, it's bureaucratic. A local effort, working with mana whenua to build a simple walking track to the beach, has dragged on, with demands for engineering investigations, weed control and traffic management plans, environmental impact surveys, maps of paper roads and marginal strips and archaeological reports.

And the local bicultural agendas are equally complex, because the history of that relationship is fraught in this region. On some issues, such as sand mining just off the coast, or the proposed but much-disputed Dome Valley landfill project, or millionaire golf course developments, there are Māori voices on both sides of the arguments. Te Rohe o Ngāti Manuhiri oversees the area with a Settlement Trust Board created when the Crown reached agreement with the iwi in 2012, granting $9 million and control over land, buildings, hill summit, riverbed and forest areas. Local hapū also control access to the beach, which they exercised rigorously during Covid-19 lockdowns. Long before that, though, in 1983, there were headlines in the *New Zealand Herald* when

Māori landowners fenced off access to the beach and began charging visitors a $1 entry fee, collected by locals on horseback. A front-page photo showed a smiling, bikini-clad guardian next to the sign proclaiming Pakiri Beach to be private property. The image defined the attitude and anger of many Aucklanders for decades. In 2010, another *Herald* story reprinted the photo again, with the headline 'Local action created a lasting legacy'. Ngāti Wai Trust Board chair Laly Haddon recalled the event, saying, in a rather understated way, that the charge drew mixed reaction but had a lasting effect since the beach was becoming polluted with so many visitors. 'I think, with our protection, it's become the beautiful beach that it has.'

The riverside land up from the beach hasn't become so beautiful. It was once covered with a massive kauri forest, the trees so densely packed that when one was felled it was held up by the surrounding canopy. The riverside sawmill produced timber taken away in barges for the Auckland housing market and kauri roof shingles, hand split in their thousands by a legendary team of young women. No trace of that forest remains. Local farms eke out a living on the erosion-prone hills. The only subdivision in the area has stalled because the land keeps slipping away. All of that gives the Pākehā presence an ambiguous foothold. And watching over this uneasy interaction is the pā site of Kiri, the chief who gave the place its name and now looks down from the hill above.

That lingering presence is everywhere in Pakiri, from both sides of its bicultural story. Pākehā settlers have found it a hard place to chop, dig and live their way into. Farmers haven't made fortunes here over four generations of toil, and family tragedy. Memories of debt, suicide, dysfunction and tragedy are hidden away in the corners – what I call in a poem 'buried talismans of livelier and deadlier times':

> *You walk by ramshackle remains of fruit packing sheds,*
> *cow bails, hay barns, a petrol pump*
> *a chimney stack and front doorstep*
> *of a long gone home that once burst with children.*
> *The ruins hold stories of families that flourished*
> *and farms that endured against*
> *floods, fires, droughts, epidemics*
> *and the killer blade of two world wars …*

As a place for exploring what Pākehā identity is all about in the twenty-first century, Pakiri is the ideal school of hard knocks. Personally, I would have preferred to find a softer bed to muse from, but living here forces me to look harder at the myths and assumptions that shape my attempts to be bicultural. It's a hard place for newcomers to belong. The Pākehā settler families who have farmed here for 150 years aren't much interested in us, simply raising a finger of acknowledgement, not insult, from a passing quad bike. Māori newcomers without connection to the local hapū don't find it easy either. Belonging takes a while.

All of this breeds a stripped-down version of Pākehā identity, light years away from the Canterbury kind, and harder edged than what we'd known in Waiapu. But this is where we chose to dig in, and so we did, walking the village and waiting to see what happened. And after a year or three, much did. The partnership with Māori isn't as harsh as I may have made it sound. It's well splashed with generosity and delight. Sometimes I can't see that for looking. As I write this, I forget to see the vase full of flax flowers, a gift from a weaving hui at the local hall, run by Te Whānau o Pakiri. 'Come and join us, both of you. Why don't you write about it?' said the organisers. Liz joined the weavers and loved it. I didn't get around to writing about it until now. And there are the numerous times we've been given fish and shellfish, food and homekill meat by Māori families, some of whom have little of their own. One kuia makes a point of sending me home a sandwich or three left over from afternoon teas at the hall. 'You need to keep your strength up,' she says. The little village provides renewing energy in so many ways. After some challenging bouts with cancer and other afflictions, something as simple as a walk up the road, gradually longer each day, has been incredibly healing.

And it's in Pakiri that I slowly relearn the rituals of yet another face of Pākehā culture, the rural brand, as different from Auckland's or Christchurch's, as night from day. It's about being backward in coming forward for a while, waiting till you're welcomed before assuming you will be, keeping out of each other's way, being generous with food when there are occasions to share it, pitching in when things go wrong in the village. Going with the flow. Like I had to with the local farmer who stopped his quad bike to tell me that he'd heard my dog was called August and didn't think that was any sort of bloody name for a dog. Not, well, dignified enough for a proper dog. (I'm not sure he thought a Jack Russell qualified as a dog at all.) I thanked him for his advice and asked him, deadpan because I already knew, what he called his horse. Milo, he told me. Call any animal Milo in the middle of any city I've ever lived in and you'd have people wondering about you. Out here it's perfectly acceptable.

Rural Pākehā culture expects you to know how to do stuff – practical things that townies pay other people to do for them and never have to learn – cleaning the filter on the septic pump, scooping dead birds out of the water tank, clearing the gutters and, above all, mowing the lawns properly. There's a right way to set levels and a wrong way. It's done in Pakiri in a range of styles, from suburban prim and trim to rustic rough – with the cutting blade set high and no thought of collecting the clippings. Spraying draws an equally wide range of methods, from organic caution to chemical blitz, with bad-tempered neighbour clashes between the two extremes. But some sort of intervention is reluctantly approved by most; otherwise the privet, thistles, ragwort and kikuyu grass would swallow us all.

This urban/rural cultural divide, which I learnt first in Nūhaka and rediscovered in Pakiri, is wider and older than I ever realised – and wider, I imagine, for Māori than Pākehā. The huge post-war migration from the countryside to the cities was a seismic shift for Māori. They became an urban people inside a generation. But Pākehā were always largely urban: most lived and worked in towns, even though the economy was based on farming the countryside. But, oddly, even for the most urbanised New Zealanders, their dreams and images of who they think they are still draw heavily on country life. Clean, green, 100 per cent pure, organically grown, smelling fresh, tasting natural – the language is loaded in favour of rural every time, even in the middle of the city. You might expect, then, that more and more people would be moving out into rural communities, but the population flow is still into the cities. Even farmers often retire to town after a lifetime on the land, and the average stay of lifestyle-block owners is only about three years before they sell up and head back to suburbs.

Going country for most New Zealanders remains a nice idea best confined to a weekend drive or a camping trip at Christmas; an image to relish, preferably in high definition colour on a big screen, rather than an actual experience. As a later convert to rural life, I can understand that romantic distancing, especially in the middle of winter when our rural paradise is mottled by excesses of mud, possum attacks and blocked drains. But on a good day when the sun is glinting off the leaves of the trees that encircle us and I look across at the dark patches of bush on the blue green hills, knowing they hold so many stories of the people of the land and the settler farmers and who have gone before me here, I can't think where else I would rather be.

But however urbanised Pākehā culture becomes as it continues to evolve, it is always going to have a taste of country, and there lies fertile ground to share with and understand Māori. Maybe our best hope for finding a just and joyful future together is to all become environmentalists. Not just brown or white but green together, in a pest-free, carbon neutral, replanted and detoxed landscape.

* * *

There's nowhere better in Pakiri for thinking about what it means to be Pākehā than walking on the beach. In that marvellous movie about the English painter J.M.W. Turner, the artist, played by Timothy Spall, scrubs out his finished canvas in a fit of fury and creative energy before starting all over again to produce a new masterpiece of light and colour. It still depicts the same place as the original work, but his inspired brush has brought about a transformation. I think of that scene when I walk on Pakiri Beach the morning after a big storm. I never fail to be stunned by the depth and scale of nature's makeover. The wind has eroded and reconfigured the beach itself into new slopes and hollows, and the sandhills behind have been carved out and steepened into unfamiliar forms. Is this really the same beach – and whose beach is it anyway?

The question isn't a new one. It was Queen Victoria, back in 1840, who instructed Hobson to ensure that the new colony's infrastructure included places for the 'recreation and amusement of the inhabitants'. She didn't specifically mention what became, in 1892, the Queen's Chain, a strip of Crown land above the high-water mark, which was reserved and couldn't be sold. But

Māori land wasn't owned by the Crown so it couldn't be reserved, and a host of other exceptions have followed. For all that, some 70 per cent of our coastline is still in public ownership and New Zealanders have increasingly high expectations that it will remain so. Witness the troubles faced by the Ports of Auckland when they attempted to encroach further into Waitematā Harbour. Queen Victoria would not have been amused by the way that saga presumes to say whose harbour it is.

Legally, the status quo regarding the ownership question is set by the 2011 Marine and Coastal Area Act, not a title that is front of mind as you wander along the sand, but vital nonetheless, since it guarantees the right of every New Zealander to free public access. The legislation was a juggling act that reshaped the balance of power in our Parliament. It proclaimed that the foreshore and seabed, the subject of bitter dispute back in 2004, belonged to no one, declaring it a 'no ownership zone' on the one hand, but restoring the right of iwi, like Ngāti Manuhiri, to seek customary use and title through the courts.

For Māori and Pākehā alike, the beach is a place of dreams – of the portal to moana nui, the enchanted world of waka and ancestors stretching across ocean and time, or of later migrations in sailing ships from the other side of the world. And the beach is the boundary, the only boundary, between us, Māori and Pākehā, and those overseas. And for all the ways we divide ourselves from each other in this country, the beach remains the edge we all share, the edge of what sets us apart from the rest of the world.

I'm also reminded, as I walk on Pakiri Beach, that it's shared territory and has always been so. It's shared with everyone who uses and sometimes abuses this space, such as the barges that scoop up sand just beyond the waves and dump it on city beaches down the coast, all somehow with the consent of council and environmental experts. My freedom to enjoy the beach is constrained by these other users. I don't mean the wider cultural constraints imposed by a rāhui when someone is drowned, or an epidemic is ravaging, or the shellfish are threatened, or, worse still, when the oil spill offshore clots up the sand and poisons the sea life. I mean the surfers and swimmers and fishers and four-wheel-drive vehicles that I have to accommodate, the areas flagged off by surf lifesavers and DOC-defined breeding grounds for birds – even the film crews that hired the sand for a day and ask me to stay out of shot as they set up cameras and actors for a British lottery ad.

One of the most important measures of how liveable and sustainable New Zealand can become as a bicultural nation depends on the partnerships we work out for enjoying the beach. That will mean treading softly where we walk on the sand.

PART II

WHERE WE ARE

CHAPTER 12

The inflammatory debate

Paul Reeves used to tell the story of the Māori bus driver who took passengers on tours of nineteenth-century battle sites in the Far North. After several stops, one of the Pākehā passengers asked the driver, 'How come when you tell the story of the fights, the Māori win every time?' The driver looked him over and said, 'So long as I'm driving this bus, that's the way it's going to be.'

The debate raging in mainstream media, and even more heatedly on social media, is just about as partisan as that, with accusations of racism flung about like confetti. On one single morning not so many months ago, RNZ carried four stories in a row on its website. Two were about local body name calling. The deputy mayor of South Waikato was accusing a fellow councillor of German descent of following in the footsteps of his 'hereditary forebears', who ignored the norms of 'decent society'. In Masterton, the deputy mayor labelled his detractors 'grumpy old, white men'. TVNZ had to accept a broadcasting standards complaint that its use of the term 'gypsy day', to refer to the date on which dairy sharemilkers move around the country, was a racial slur against the Romany community. And Disney's streaming platform updated its content advisory notice on racism to include *Dumbo* (for its depiction of the crows, one of whom is named Jim), and *The Jungle Book* (for King Louie the ape, shown to be lazy and singing Dixie jazz).

To interpret why the debates about racism become so incendiary, a little context is needed. Behind the ranting and raving lies much that is highly formalised and carefully constructed. The skill of talking to each other is one part art, two parts science. It's the ancient science of rhetoric – persuasive speaking. European settlers came to New Zealand at a time when rhetoric was dropping off the higher education syllabus in Britain, but here in Aotearoa, the art of persuasive oratory was highly prized on marae, as it still is today. The way that Māori talk about Pākehā in formal settings is artful compared with the way in which some Pākehā bang on about Māori in Facebook taunts and talkback radio harangues.

The racially different dialogues rarely overlap. Few Pākehā hear what Māori are saying about them except for the occasional outburst that is picked up by the media, such as the taunts at the time of Tuia 250, the government-sponsored commemoration for the 250th anniversary of the arrival of HMS *Endeavour* in Aotearoa in 1769–70, labelling Cook a 'syphilitic destroyer of indigenous cultures, a barbarian and a racist', or Donna Awatere Huata's since revised but never forgotten call for Pākehā to 'go home'. By comparison, the Pākehā rhetoric about Māori is vastly more visible and extreme.

At the inflammatory end of the scale are two organisations. Hobson's Pledge was created and is led by former National Party leader Don Brash to oppose and eliminate any trace of racial preference in the way the country is run. It promotes a mistranslation of Governor Hobson's pledge at Waitangi for Māori and Pākehā to be 'one people'. The One New Zealand Foundation was established in 1988 to fight what it calls 'Māori apartheid' and promote 'one law, one flag, one New Zealand' and the dismantling of the Waitangi Tribunal. Its best-known advocate is Northland farmer Allan Titford, whose long-running dispute with Māori over land ownership was overtaken by his conviction for rape, assault and arson in 2013 when he was jailed for 24 years. Both organisations' websites peddle conspiracy theories about such subjects as creeping Marxist ideology, conspiracies about lost versions of the treaty, secretive Waitangi Tribunals and a red-haired, pale-skinned tribe, most likely from Wales, predating Māori 3000 years ago.

Forming a supporting chorus to these websites are the shock jocks, the talkback radio hosts who assure us that 'Māori were very lucky they got the Brits' as their colonisers. Then there are letters circulating online, decrying, for example, the 'Māori cultural takeover and the greed, waste and hostility' that go with it. There is also the New Zealand Centre for Political Research, originally the New Zealand Centre for Political Debate, founded by former ACT Party politician Muriel Newman, which describes itself as having 'a research-based approach to public policy matters' and encouraging 'the free and open debate of political issues'. It hosts Karl du Fresne, former editor of the *Dominion Post*, who has written that 'in the 21st century the word racist simply means anyone who doesn't conform to the authoritarian orthodoxies of identity politics'.

In 2021, historian and former Labour minister Michael Bassett wrote a newspaper article, later deleted and apologised for by the publisher, that, in the words of a reasoned and thorough response from Scott Hamilton, maintained that 'a cabal of "Māori revolutionaries", "woke" academics, and civil servants is working with sinister efficiency to turn Aotearoa New Zealand into a bicultural dystopia'. Brash criticised the removal of Bassett's piece, claiming that the decision showed 'how far New Zealand has drifted' in the wrong direction.

Accounts of warmongering by Māori (talk about the pot calling the kettle black) are endlessly recycled – the Musket Wars are popular in this line of argument – but nothing is mentioned about their peacemaking, which happened even more frequently. Accusations flow about bloodthirsty Māori back in a time when Europeans were still hanging, drawing and quartering offenders. We hear a lot about the warrior excesses of Te Rauparaha but much less about the peacemaking missions of his son Tamihana, who sought to heal the damage caused by his father's campaigns in Canterbury.

And then there are the simple mistranslations of Māori words, skewed to suit a political agenda. The famous phrase Hobson is reputed to have used at the signing of the treaty in Waitangi, 'He iwi tahi tātou', is a prime example. To translate that as 'We are now one people' is to use the wrong pronoun. It's an easy mistake to make, given that there are some 27 different possessive pronouns in te reo, but the endlessly repeated mistake – as mentioned above, Hobson's Pledge is a major offender – is driven more by political than grammatical motives. When Ngāpuhi elder Waihoroi Shortland translated the phrase for the Governor General Patsy Reddy at Waitangi in 2020, he said it meant 'Together we are one nation.'

At the other end of the scale is the disconcerted but never publicly voiced disquiet of older, middle-class Pākehā, who would like to be sympathetic but fear the claims for self-determination, such as those seen in *He Puapua*, the *Report of a Working Group on a Plan to Realise the UN Declaration on the Rights of Indigenous Peoples in Aotearoa/New Zealand*, and the growing use of te reo are a step too far. The dis-ease isn't confined to conservative quarters. An opinion piece on the *Listener*'s editorial page echoed those fears, complaining about 'untranslated, rapidly spoken Māori, particularly on radio' leaving older people, especially, 'feeling excluded and belittled'.

The language employed across this range of views about Māori contains some dominant narratives, as the linguists call them, familiar and popular themes that are often repeated but rarely fact-checked or updated. 'They've never had it so good' gets a lot of coverage. It's often coupled with a comparison with other colonised peoples such as Aboriginal Australians. Then there's: 'The problems all happened a long time ago and it's not my fault. Don't blame me for my great-grandparents' mistakes.'

And yes, 'Māori had it tough but it's time to kiss and make up and move on.' Actually, some say, 'The Crown is doing its best, just look at the treaty settlements so far. It all takes time.' 'Yes, there's racism, but it's not as bad as it used to be. We're making good progress.' Frequent, too, are complaints about the sense of entitlement that many Māori have: 'It's as though we and the government owe them something more.' The Treaty of Waitangi is a good thing to have, 'but we're making too much of it, much more than what it meant in 1840. I'm sure it meant something different back then.'

All these narratives – and I've excluded the more obviously racist and crude ones about genetic and cultural inferiority – are repeated over and over by people who seem to have no awareness at all about their own privilege, their own impatience when they don't get the justice and respect to which they feel entitled. And when figures are flung around about the cost of compensation and restoration, we don't look for fair comparisons. As a 2018 Stuff article pointed out, citing Treasury and Office of Treaty Settlements figures, of the $1322 billion of government spending from 1993 to that point, just $2.24 billion had been spent on treaty settlement redress, less than the $2.5 billion budget of the Auckland District Health Board for the 2019–20 year.

The 1998 Ngāi Tahu settlement amounted to $170 million. The economic losses to the iwi as a result of the Crown's land purchases were valued at more than $20 billion. When Pākehā feel under pressure from Māori, their collective memory of the worst moments in their own history becomes ever more selective and they can begin to feel like victims who are being blamed unfairly and excessively. And because Pākehā are the dominant culture responsible for so much damage, there is nothing they can say in their own defence. They have to wait for Māori to do that.

Older Māori frequently point out that they were prevented from speaking te reo in school. The Native Schools Act of 1867 required English to be used wherever practicable and though te reo wasn't officially banned, it was widely discouraged and students who used it were often strapped or caned. The trauma that created has left a legacy of whakamā (shame) and called for a formal apology from the Crown. In Nūhaka, the story is more nuanced. Te reo was taught in school over 60 years ago, and back in the early 1900s students had to speak English but were also taught formal Māori grammar. But the suppression of the language is remembered as if it had just happened. And Pākehā shouldn't be surprised: the pain and insult of such a denial of culture takes generations to ease.

Comparisons between our different cultures over who is the least cruel or the most destructive, to say nothing of who is smarter or braver, end up taking us nowhere and should never serve as excuses for bad behaviour. When I see derogatory references to so-called 'Stone Age' Māori culture, I think of the ancient navigational and seafaring skills for ocean voyaging that culture sustained, stretching back to a time when European sailors were still keeping in sight of land for fear of tipping off the edge of the world.

But are all Pākehā criticisms of Māori explained by a deep-seated and deliberate racism? There's an institutional form of racism that anyone who is privileged inherits and expresses without stopping to think about it. And that racism is built into the forms and habits of the language Pākehā use every day. Most Pākehā people of goodwill have never fact-checked what they say about Māori, never asked them how it feels to be on the receiving end of stereotypes and insults, even if they're unintended. I grew up with prolific unspoken assumptions about what Māori were 'naturally' good at doing. Well-meaning people told me that they made good drivers, of bulldozers especially, for some reason. They were great musicians – they were the best guitarists – and soldiers, of course, and politicians, nurses, even doctors. But scientists? Probably not. Nor businessmen either, because they had too many friends and relatives they were obliged to take care of. They could be persuaded to sell you anything, provided you paid them on the spot in cash.

These throwaway lines, these memes, are used unthinkingly by otherwise well-intentioned people, as casually as online help desks ask us 'How's your day going?' The cheap labels remain in place until they're rubbed out by personal experience, academic research and, best of all, getting to know enough Māori to discover they don't fit stereotypes any more easily than Pākehā do. But in a society that increasingly isolates Māori through inequality, the sort of cross-cultural contact that erases these distortions becomes harder to find.

CHAPTER 13

Trying to talk to each other

Good communication isn't rocket science. There are some things that just have to happen in order to achieve mutual respect and understanding. There won't be justice if the givers and receivers of it aren't talking. And that can't be forced, because New Zealand is a community not a courtroom, as we've been learning all over again in recent attempts to legislate against hate speech.

Some components of good communication are as basic and essential as the nuts that hold a wheel to an axle. For instance, Pākehā need channels they can trust. Māori have those through tradition and whakapapa, forms of oratory, chant and song; respecting the rules of how things are said and who does the talking. Using those time-tested channels ensures authenticity and determines what is heard and believed collectively. The Pākehā world, however, is much more individualised. Its channels are less anchored in local cultures and traditions, and increasingly driven by technology and social media. Facebook, Twitter, TikTok and text messages are rapidly becoming the prime vehicles for the exchange of cross-cultural images. The stereotypes are multiplied online without any check on accuracy or fairness.

The different channels aren't exclusive to any one culture. Young Māori and Pākehā alike relish their phones and devices. What's needed are channels that both cultures can trust: musical forms like hip hop, art forms like weaving and carving, performing arts like dance and kapa haka, sporting codes like waka ama and rugby and league. Only by finding channels both can trust will Māori and Pākehā stop talking past each other.

Communication obviously requires a receiver as well as a sender. Communication theory talks about a receiver in terms of anticipation, and a sender in terms of intention. You may think you're sending a message but it's never more than a fond hope until it's received and understood. Radio traffic rules require you to say those words out loud, but we take that for granted in our ordinary everyday conversation, then wonder why no one seems to be listening. And the receiver will only ever take our message on board if he or she is expecting it, is ready and willing to receive it.

The Pākehā history of attempts at cross-cultural communication, especially regarding health and education, is filled with messages that went nowhere. And Māori calls for self-determination, respect for sacred places, for tapu and rāhui, and the simplest of courtesies such as endorsement by elders, are constantly ignored. What Māori and Pākehā expect from and intend for each other is still, 200 years on, a conversation that's only beginning. The real intentions of senders remain suspect. Receivers don't expect much. Channels aren't checked to be loud and clear.

And when Pākehā do succeed in communicating, it's because they've taken the trouble to weigh up the response from their partner. The successful ventures in co-governance, the emergence of a Māori Health Authority/Te Mana Hauora Māori, a school curriculum that embraces a shared history – all these reflect years of Māori and Pākehā listening to each other, building trust in each other's good intentions and expecting good things from each other. When one good conversation leads to another and another, when both sides start to feel that they're taking each other's differences seriously, even when they can't agree, then communication happens and a track record of trust is built up.

As the rhetoric ramps up, so does the need for Pākehā to analyse the weight of the words they use. Speaking at Waitangi in 2006, Hone Kaa put it like this: 'It's good that you Pākehā are who you are, and it's important that you know who you are. But you need to understand how you are and who you are – and how powerfully you are who you are.' When Pākehā start to weigh the power of the words they speak, and the effect they have when they speak about Māori, then a truly shared society will emerge ever more quickly. But it will involve learning some rules for the conversation, such as who can speak and when.

* * *

Children used to be brought up to speak when they were spoken to. Elders used to have the floor first. Māori women on the marae are still expected to defer to male speakers, though it is the women who speak first in the karanga calling on the visitors.

The rules that govern public speech are complex and changing. New protocols emerge. It's happening in the way Pākehā and Māori speak to and about each other.

When you're welcomed onto a marae as a Pākehā with only a modicum of te reo, there's absolutely no question about who gets to talk and when, and, if you're female, whether you speak at all. You may, or maybe not, have someone alongside you willing to translate what's being said (and sometimes laughed) about you, and eventually be invited to respond. It's a bracingly humbling experience to be rendered speechless and uncomprehending, and for many Pākehā, just a little terrifying. I sometimes wonder whether Māori don't rather enjoy Pākehā discomfort. After all, it's one of the very few times where they're totally in control and able to set all the rules for cross-cultural encounter. Maybe there's a bit of emotional rebalancing and catch-up going on, making up for all the times Māori have been left awkward and embarrassed in a Pākehā-dominated world.

My sense, and it's only a sense, is that Pākehā are behaving and speaking more cautiously around Māori than they ever have before. They know how easy it is to offend and how often that has happened in the past through stereotypes, jokes and assumptions that once went unchallenged, but are now labelled racist. And for Pākehā to argue they didn't mean what they said to be racist is about as helpful as telling the driver of the car you've crashed into that you weren't looking.

Pākehā see TV pictures of homeless Māori sleeping in their cars and ask, under their breath, why they don't get a job. They read court reports of young Māori offenders being sentenced on assault charges and say to themselves they deserve that and more. And Māori watched with disbelief the plans, later abandoned, to spend $785 million on a new Auckland Harbour cycle bridge. They surely compared the police response to Lycra-clad protest cyclists with their treatment of leather-clad gang riders and wondered about parallel universes.

Once in a while there's a public outburst trumpeted across the media – a racist insult shouted at a sporting event, a Twitter rant that goes viral, a politician's aside that colonialism wasn't really so bad. There's a brief hullabaloo and threats to involve the race relations commissioner, but the public exchanges evaporate quickly and the insults go underground. Some dreamers in the Pākehā world imagine that these cross-cultural tensions will simply fade away, once the most glaring inequalities have been solved, but the chances are they'll get worse, because underlying them are mutual disrespect and lack of trust. Barrister, solicitor and academic Ani Mikaere puts it bluntly: 'Pākehā have to trust Māori not to behave as badly as they have done since arriving in our country.' Pākehā don't belong here on their terms. Like it or not, they are in a state of co-dependency, however much both partners claim to be independent, self-sufficient, even sovereign. As Michael Grimshaw says, 'I am a Pākehā because I live in a Māori country.' Can Pākehā and Māori learn to talk to each other as though that's true? To achieve that, Pākehā will need to be at least as clear about who they are as Māori are about themselves.

CHAPTER 14

Invisibility's fine – subscribe to mine

It's too easy to stop seeing. As Gary Younge put it in a piece for the *Guardian*, 'Inured to the obvious, the familiar becomes banal and ultimately invisible even as it stands in plain sight.' He quoted James Kirkpatrick, writing in the early 1960s about southern white Americans' attachment to racial segregation: 'Who hears a clock tick or the surf murmur or the train pass? Not those who live by the clock, or the sea, or the train.' Māori might not have been surprised about their invisibility in Pākehā eyes. After all, they thought the first white people they saw had eyes in the back of their heads. Why else would the sailors on those first sailing ships row their boats ashore with their backs facing the way they were heading?

For the first 40 or so years of Pākehā settlement, Māori were seen, of course. As the dominant culture driving the economy in peacetime and, later at war, they could hardly be avoided. But then as Pākehā culture took over and built a largely urban-based presence, Māori were increasingly marginalised – economically, culturally and in sheer physical presence. They became largely invisible, as they still are outside the Far North, South Auckland, Rotorua and Gisborne. In the wealthy suburbs of Remuera, Karori, Fendalton and, ironically, Māori Hill in Dunedin, the closest you probably get to te ao Māori is a programme on Māori Television or a broadcast of an All Black or Super Rugby game. Māori make up 15.6 per cent of the population but you have to go looking to find them in urban New Zealand or the Canterbury hill country – anywhere, in fact, that is halfway affluent.

After two centuries and more of living together on the same islands, you'd think Māori and Pākehā would have got to know each other. And they did for those first few decades, until the governor of the day made them antagonists in battle, then punished Māori for daring to 'rebel' and began the long process of legal dispossession. Nothing was ever the same after that and the two cultures ended up knowing less and less about each other and living further and further apart. And when Māori increasingly joined Pākehā in towns and cities from the 1950s, it was as less advantaged, poorer cousins. On every indicator from health status to educational achievement, prison numbers to housing, the gap grew wider.

The history of how all that happened wasn't taught at any level of the education system. You had to be a specialist historian to learn about the way native land ownership was redefined as individual rather than corporate title, way back in 1862, how 3,000,000 acres (1,215,000 hectares) were confiscated as punishment in the following year, and that Māori seats – just four, when on a population basis it should have been 20 – were established in 1867 to prevent Māori gaining a majority in Parliament. And if that wasn't enough, in 1877 Chief Justice Sir James Prendergast – the same judge who sanctioned the invasion of Parihaka – declared the Treaty of Waitangi 'worthless' because the signatories had been 'a civilised nation and a group of savages'. The treaty had not been made a part of the country's domestic law, and so it amounted to a 'simple nullity'. It took another 100 years to reverse that decision.

Once it became clear that Māori weren't going to die out, as many expected at the end of the nineteenth century, they were gradually accepted, on condition that they were assimilated and made to be like Pākehā. Māori language was discouraged in schools, Māori knowledge devalued and ignored, Māori soldiers were not permitted to go to war in the same way Pākehā could (until 1939). Māori could play rugby, but not always overseas or only as honorary whites. All those conditions, and a thousand more unspoken, served to hide te ao Māori from Pākehā eyes and ears. And because Pākehā didn't see that world, let alone engage with it, they didn't feel involved in what was going on for the people who lived inside it.

Some saw the problems, even at the time. It was in the 1950s, for instance, that Presbyterian minister John Laughton said, 'To try and make Māori into Pākehā like some plant is to strip him of every leaf and bud and leave him a gaunt and naked stem.' But he and others like him were the exception and the powers that be continued to promote assimilation and make it acceptable. In 1980 the Human Rights Commission was still singing the same song, declaring that 'being a Māori is often a state of mind' and because there was 'so little Māori blood involved we should all be called New Zealanders … the majority of Māori consider themselves New Zealanders and are quite happy to live with the rest of us.' And in the same year, Minister of Māori Affairs Ben Couch declared, 'I am a New Zealander first and a Māori second. We are living in a Pākehā world, and if I were to rely on the Māoris for a living I would starve.' He would have found many to agree with him in Nūhaka.

Assimilation was widely seen as inevitable, and even some academics agreed. Peter Munz, who became Professor of History at Victoria University of Wellington in 1968, well before that institution felt compelled to add a Māori name, declared that 'Assimilation and colonisation are the essence of human history. You can try to stop it or slow it down but you can't prevent it, no matter what you do.' And few would have disagreed with his claim that 'Pākehā have ceased to be all that English and Māori will eventually cease to be all that Māori'.

I've been told through my life that I'm too tall, too scared, that I can't run fast enough or tackle hard enough. But I've never been told that my skin is the wrong colour or been forbidden to use the name my family gave me. I can't imagine what that would be like. Especially if someone decided to call me something they found easier to pronounce or replaced it altogether with something they thought was more civilised. With a surname like Bluck, I've often been told, much to my annoyance, how odd it is and what it rhymes with. But no one has ever asked me Malcolm X's famous question, 'Who taught you to hate the colour of your skin?' And I've never been punished for using the language my parents taught me.

Until very recently I'd never thought of myself as being especially privileged. I thought that word meant coming from a family with a lot of money or going to a school fancier than mine, which I didn't want to attend anyway. Being Pākehā never limited the access I had to the courses I wanted to take, the job I dreamt of doing, the flat I wanted to rent. And the family history I inherit, though it has a few dodgy bits, has never made me feel angry, ashamed or resentful. As a Pākehā student, I was never accused of being specially privileged simply because I was able to attend university, but Māori students were. And no one ever asked me, 'How Pākehā are you?' Māori friends were often asked, 'How Māori are you?' – an echo from the days when being 'mixed race' was a slur. It still happens. So when I come face to face with Māori who accuse me of being privileged for simply being who I am, I'm initially baffled and in denial, until I realise their accusation isn't so much personal, though it is that, as systemic and historical.

Auckland-based forensic psychiatrist Krishna Pillai sees this every day in his work in the criminal justice system where, in his words, 'the structural effects of colonisation are expressed in some of the worst examples of inequity in Aotearoa New Zealand'. Fifty per cent of the cases he deals with are Māori,

15 per cent are of Pacific descent. This 'gross over-representation', Pillai points out, 'is not due to the personal failings of the people involved'. For each case he draws together 'the biological, psychological, social and cultural, linking the here and now to all that has gone before' in a 'complex and interconnecting web of cause and effect.' And the 'thread of connection' goes a long way back – to 'the traumas experienced by previous generations … The experiences of our grandparents are still carried in our DNA.'

Two centuries of living together has produced some wonderful things for both cultures but the balance of those benefits is lopsided. Even the shrillest of voices that claim colonisation was good for Māori don't claim it was bad for Pākehā. On the balance of land owned, wealth accumulated, health benefits, school achievement, time spent in prison, life expectancy – almost any measure you choose – Pākehā have done better from our colonial history. And, what's more, they have controlled the way that history is told.

* * *

We've been calling each other names ever since we first met. Māori warriors thought the first Pākehā sailors they saw were goblins, which was nothing compared with the new arrivals' characterisation of Māori as smelly, painted savages – this from men who wouldn't have smelt like rosebuds themselves. They misread gestures of welcome and challenge as intents to kill and responded with musket fire.

The earliest descriptions of Māori by Pākehā were a curious mixture of fear and admiration, insult and awe. An introductory book written for new colonists in 1839–40 by the Secretary to the New Zealand Company, John Ward, described Māori as 'essentially a savage people ... dirty in their persons, and sometimes overrun with vermin', who knew almost nothing about 'the meaning of arts, trade, industry, or coin', had no roads but only footpaths and lacked any system of law or government. 'With the physical powers and passions of men,' Ward wrote, 'they have at present the intellect of children, and in moral principle, are little above the level of brute creation.' He did, however, admit that there was 'a natural politeness and grandeur in their deportment, a yearning after poetry, music, and the fine arts, a wit and eloquence', that their language was 'rich and sonorous' and that they excelled at carving.

The insults, written and visual, continued. Many popular illustrated magazines from the late nineteenth century and the first decades of the twentieth featured cartoons portraying Māori as fat, lazy and stupid, and Chinese as sinister and drug-addicted foreign devils. To modern eyes, the level of casual, unapologetic racism is startling. Terms like 'hori' and mimicry of speech like 'py corry' were commonplace, and jokes about Māori as slow and dumb, and references to keeping 'Māori time', were commonplace even into the 1960s.

The myths about Māori seem to fall into four groups: the inherently good, dignified and even noble; the bad ones who get into trouble with the law; the radical stirrers or 'haters and wreckers', as one prime minister described them; the peaceful ones happy to accept the status quo. There is also another category that divides old Māori, traditional, respectful, pliable, close to nature and mostly rural, from new Māori, who are extreme, aggressive and uncompromising. These myths still swirl about, just below the surface of public debate, distorting the conversation and preventing dialogue from being creative and respectful. They are used to brand Māori as being too Māori or not Māori enough, too willing to 'fit in' or not willing enough. These 'callous overgeneralisations', as Andrew Eruera Vercoe calls them, cause enormous hurt. 'If you're Māori,' he says, 'you're either a mealy mouthed Treaty of Waitangi, tino rangatiratanga prune head (like Moana Jackson) or you're a benefit beer drinking degenerate (any Māori leaning on a bar).' In the end these myths and stereotypes damage us all, on both the giving and the receiving end. As Vercoe eloquently puts it, 'Every time a Māori is locked up in prison, every time a Māori is denied his or her basic rights, every time a Māori assaults someone else we all, yes even Pākehā, lose a little bit of mana.'

Even the way Māori and Pākehā talk about each other is run according to Pākehā rules – in other words, in English. Psychologist Raymond Nairn has talked about 'the attempt to civilize Māori by the perfect language of English', which he believes keeps both cultures 'cribbed, cabined and confined within a Pākehā speech community'. At the heart of all this is a division over what it means to be normal.

When Pākehā first arrived in New Zealand, Māori was the measure of normality: the very word meant, literally, ordinary or normal. At home and abroad they were called the New Zealanders. Pākehā were the guests and a tiny minority at that, and until the Treaty of Waitangi was signed, they had no legal rights to even be here. But by the time Pākehā had been in New Zealand for a century or so, being normal meant speaking English, following English law, being defined by, and taking pride in, a heritage and culture that were heavily weighted towards the British. When Pākehā New Zealanders said they were going home, they often meant they were heading off on a trip to Britain. That usage has faded but many Pākehā today are genuinely puzzled over why Māori wouldn't prefer to be like them, enjoying the same privileges of middle-class life, all good Kiwis together.

Pākehā fail to understand the depth of Māori anger and alienation. How, they ask, could anyone possibly compare our colonial history to a holocaust? Equally, Māori are baffled by Pākehā inability to see what's going on. Sometimes the debate is akin to a description that a Jewish rabbi once gave me on a visit to Israel, to describe the confrontation with Palestinians and Jews. 'It's a collision,' he said, 'between two traumatised peoples.' Pākehā don't see themselves in that way, but memory loss about their history and blindness about the social condition of their partner *does* create trauma of a different sort from that experienced by Māori. And if trauma is too strong a word, then many Pākehā are at least fearful about, and certainly rattled by, the tone of the current debate.

* * *

So what exactly are Pākehā scared of? Top of the list is that the demand for Māori self-determination, tino rangatiratanga, will result in two separate societies, a new kind of apartheid. Take the reaction to the *He Puapua* report. You could be forgiven for thinking this discussion document on improving race relations by 2040 was written by the devil himself, given the panicked attacks by some Pākehā commentators and politicians.

There's nothing in the report that hasn't been heard before. The idea of an upper parliamentary house to protect Māori interests has been long advocated by all sorts of political parties and organisations, including the Anglican Church. And the idea of a parallel court system floated in the report is already being used in some places. Co-governance models, another suggestion, are already working in conservation estates. Both National and Labour governments have advocated shared leadership in such programmes as Whānau Ora, and social investment and primary healthcare models that target the most vulnerable. The reforms of Oranga Tamariki are all about self-determining governance.

Back in the 1840s, Selwyn, Colenso and Grace, to name only three missionaries, called for different constitutional self-governing structures for Māori, leasing rather than selling land, even a separate parliamentary house for Māori. To label self-determination as a new form of separatism or apartheid is to ignore history and forget the distinctive compact on which New Zealand is founded.

Another fear is that Māori language and culture will bury that of Pākehā. That, to demonstrate respect, Pākehā will be required to speak te reo, sing waiata at every public event, join in a haka – and because they don't know how to do any of those things properly, they'll humiliate themselves. That Māori poverty will get priority over that afflicting Pākehā. That Māori will get to be even more entitled and privileged than Pākehā are. For a culture that has enjoyed privilege and priority, dominated language and cultural choices for so long, all these fears speak more about projection than real threat. The deepest fear might be that Māori might not be as good to Pākehā as Pākehā think they've been to Māori.

Trust is the nub of the issue, and being honest with each other when that trust breaks down, as it has over and over again. Professor Ranginui Walker often described our history as the settlers acting from the start as if sovereignty over the land had been ceded with the treaty, and Māori acting as though they had never given it away. Commenting on that same bewilderment when speaking at a Turakina Māori Girls' College prizegiving in 1997, Professor Hirini Moko Mead described the Pākehā before the Second World War as 'a mixed up sort of fellow. His body belonged to New Zealand but his soul belonged to a little island somewhere else'. And although they were now 'eating our food, putting our history into textbooks and claiming Māori art as New Zealand art', Mead regarded the huge majority of Pākehā, though sympathetic, as 'still to be persuaded that Māori have a right to be different from them'. A more recent comment came in

2015 from Tipa Mahuta of the Waikato Regional Council: 'For 150 years we've been walking around each other and we're still a bit of a mystery to each other.' Any other marriage in which the partners continued to remain such a mystery to each other would have failed long ago. But we're still together, well sort of. And as Archbishop Whakahuihui Vercoe used to love to say, 'Like it or not, we're stuck with each other.'

Growing up in a Māori village, I knew there was something distinctive and different about that culture – in the way food was prepared, offered and shared, in their attitude towards old people, in the time and care they took to grieve, in the way they told stories. When I asked a Māori friend what he personally thought about something, and he answered with a sentence that always began not with 'I' but 'we', I thought he was being evasive. And even though I lived in a Māori village, an invitation to a Māori home was a rare event for a Pākehā boy. And when I did, I knew I was in different territory, welcomed with an unhurried and generous hospitality that was not the same as I encountered in Pākehā homes.

At the beginning of European settlement, Pākehā lived in Māori houses, or rough copies of them at least. As quickly as possible they built their own, which looked more and more like the ones they'd left behind in Europe. And over the next 100 years Māori abandoned their traditional housing forms for European ones, increasingly defined by regulations and building codes, and as the land they were allowed to build on shrank through confiscation and dispossession. All this was done perfectly legally: the 1862 Native Lands Act that individualised Māori title (thereby making more land available for Pākehā settlers), a series of huge land confiscations through the early 1860s to punish 'rebellious' natives, the 1865 Native Land Court Act that confiscated any ownership that wasn't defended in court. Māori freedom to live where and how they chose was enormously constrained.

To lose your house is everyone's nightmare, because a house is not simply a physical dwelling but an emotional and spiritual space to inhabit, where you are free to be who you are, where you can feel 'at home'. No wonder we hesitate before sharing houses with strangers. It requires something as intense and intimate as a marriage or a long friendship to make it work. Where you live is powerfully entangled with who you are. Names and addresses go together.

The address of the country as a whole has also caused problems. Aotearoa as a name is held to be a trendy recent invention, even though it was widely used in the nineteenth century by Governor Grey and King Tāwhiao alike. The King Movement, often meeting in a Waikato village called Aotearoa, certainly helped to popularise its use more than Niu Tireni, which was the translation used in both the 1835 Declaration of Independence by the United Tribes and the Treaty of Waitangi five years later. What's more, it features in ancient pre-European moteatea (chants). Kuramārōtini, sometimes known as Hine-te-aparangi, the wife of the great explorer Kupe, is said to have cried out, when she, her husband and the tohunga, Pekahourangi, first glimpsed a cloud-covered land mass, 'He ao! He ao! He Aotea!' To turn this into a political choice between a traditional Māori name and one dropped off by a passing Dutch explorer centuries later is silly and inflammatory. But because the matter has become so politicised, it might be wise to use both names for the country and let opinion evolve and consensus settle, as it rapidly is already. To ban the English name right now will only serve to sour things further.

CHAPTER 15

Call me by my name

Compared with Pākehā, Māori are very clear about where they belong and who they are collectively. They never have to debate what to call themselves as Māori, iwi by iwi. Pākehā, by contrast, is an ambivalent name. Newspaper polls vary widely but suggest that only about half of us at best are comfortable using it. But would those who dislike the name be happy with any name given to them by Māori? Is it more about not feeling that any special name is needed?

The term has suffered from rumours that it began as a swear word attributed to a prominent Māori politician who frequented Bellamy's bar. The rumours grew into claims that the word really means flea, rat or, best of all, a transliteration of 'bugger ya'. Branko Marcetic has traced this history of misuse and the campaigns back in the 1980s by the Jaycees and some National Party branches to ban the name. The government census forms have reflected that same ambivalence. Pākehā as a category was added in 1996, then removed after the outcry in 2001, replaced by 'New Zealander' in 2006 and then removed again. In the

2018 census, around 15,000 people chose to write 'Pākehā' rather than tick the category 'New Zealand European'. *Jacobin* magazine writer Branko Marcetic estimates about 15 per cent of the population use the word, which is 'still contested but increasingly accepted as a mainstream term'. In 2013 the New Zealand Attitudes and Values Study, which surveys thousands of New Zealanders annually on a wide range of topics, found 'no evidence whatsoever' that the term Pākehā symbolised any negative attitudes towards New Zealanders of European descent. In fact, as one of the researchers pointed out, the choice by Māori to use the term was linked to how strongly they identify as Māori.

In simplest terms, Pākehā is no more than a description of one of the new arrivals who came from the sea, or perhaps, with tongue in cheek, an abbreviation of pakepakehā – the mythical and mischievous creatures who live in the forest and come out only at night. However it began, it remains a beautifully balanced three-syllable word gifted by Māori. And to see the word as a gift makes all the difference. It involves a relationship between the giver and the receiver. In Māori lore, the giver continues to share in the benefit of a gift that's been given. By accepting the name, we accept a connection and an ever-evolving meaning. By the mid-twentieth century Pākehā simply meant fair-skinned people who make their home here, regardless of ancestry or birthplace.

The word has its limitations for people who settle here and are not fair skinned, for the name has been dominated by people of European heritage. For those who aren't, the simplest solution seems to be to hyphenate the word and talk of Pākehā-Chinese or Pākehā-Indian. That way both heritages are honoured. But that isn't a popular solution. Pākehā is a loaded word. It implies a political and personal sympathy with Māori, a gratitude for the name as a gift and a recognition that we aren't all simply lumped together as New Zealanders. In *This Pākehā Life: An Unsettled Memoir*, Alison Jones says it means to be 'permanently oriented to Māori, to be peculiarly related here and to be knowledgeable about our historic entanglements'. To apply the name to yourself implies that you've made a choice and set a course that involves taking partnership with Māori seriously, supporting the use of te reo, trying to work out what this bicultural business is all about. You may not say any of that out loud, but that's what will be assumed, especially by those who think the word Pākehā belongs to the woke vocabulary of the try-hards and the politically correct.

For others, it simply seems like a step too far, a commitment that might need to be made one day, but not yet. Trouble is, if you're not Māori and try to avoid calling yourself anything other than Kiwi, you end up woefully oversimplifying what it means to be a bicultural and eventually a multicultural nation. To take the easy route and simply call yourself a New Zealander begs the question of what that means, because it's not a question that one partner can answer alone. It's a bit like someone naming and describing their marriage without referring to their spouse.

Back in the 1980s when the concept of Kiwiana started to flourish, we began to debate, rather earnestly and self-consciously, what it meant to be Pākehā. In 1989 the *Dominion* and *Evening Post* published a photokit for schools with defining images of Pākehāness: keeping time, obsessively measuring the weather, shaking hands, wearing ties and war medals, carrying handbags, presenting wooden keys at twenty-first birthdays, even playing with Buzzy Bees, as Prince William did in 1983, though the British press reported the toy as an Australian icon.

Then there was, also in the 1980s, Michael King's claim that Pākehā could be indigenous too, a concept that doesn't fit well in today's bicultural debate. Most Māori commentators see it as provocative and a way of trying to set up the debate on Pākehā terms, forgetting who is manuhiri and who is tangata whenua. King's claim is still attractive to many, especially Pākehā who believe their spiritual attachment to the land is as deep as that of any Māori. If you want to enrage a fifth-generation high country farmer, tell them their connection to the hills they grew up in is only skin deep.

Many people, however, fail to read on in *Being Pākehā*. 'We are not,' King wrote, 'an indigenous culture that displaces or supplants that of the tangata whenua.'

> It is in a symbiotic relationship to Māoritanga. And because it will increasingly nourish and sustain Pākehā people and enable more and more of them to feel they truly belong in this part of the world – it will be a vital component in the process of Māori-Pākehā accommodation. Because Pākehā people will cease to feel threatened by the enlarging Māori

presence in New Zealand when they have begun to feel whole and to feel secure. The proponents of white backlash are those who are not whole, and who feel anything but secure.

More than 30 years on, those words have a prophetic edge as Pākehā react angrily not only to a growing Māori presence but also to an ever stronger and sharper voice on everything from water rights to control of prisons, healthcare and beaches.

* * *

So how might this identity become more attractive, easier to own and a little less ambiguous? Is there a better label Pākehā could give themselves than the one Māori have provided? How can this identity be retrofitted for the new millennium, especially for those who are not Māori and whose heritage is not European?

Some ethnic groups have already done that without saying so. Consider the Dalmatian community, part of the Northland landscape since the 1880s, where they dug for kauri gum. By 1898 there were 2000 of them in the Bay of Islands district alone. Many intermarried with Māori and melded into the local culture. Like Māori they endured severe discrimination. An 1898 law removed their right to hold gum-digging licences and reserved them for British settlers. And in 1914, because they were sometimes known as Austrians – and therefore Germans by association – they were declared to be 'enemy aliens'. Yet despite all that, they thrived and helped to found the wine industry New

Zealand now boasts about to the world. Northland Dalmatians are a proud group. They could be Ngāti Dalmatians.

So, too, could Dunedin's Chinese community. With ancestors reaching back into the Otago goldfields of the 1860s, and suffering even more extreme discrimination, Chinese New Zealanders have forged their own distinctive links with Māori. The most poignant story of that bond dates back to the sinking of the SS *Ventnor* off Hokianga Harbour in 1902. The ship went down with 13 crew and the remains of 489 Chinese miners, which were being taken home to China for burial. As these remains, in their zinc-lined kauri bone-boxes, were washed ashore over the years, local iwi, Te Rarawa, Te Mahurehure and Te Roroa, gathered them up, unaware of where they came from, and buried them reverently. Much later the connections were discovered and in 2013 plaques were placed at several sites in the area to record the thanks of the Chinese for the care given by mana whenua to their ancestors. In 2020 a New Zealand Chinese Association SS *Ventnor* memorial was opened at Opononi.

Hundreds of stories celebrate life and death, flesh and blood connections between different ethnic communities and Māori; they are remembered, treasured, retold generation after generation by families at dinner tables and weddings and funerals. Differing in tone and flavour from region to region, they fit only loosely under the blanket label of Pākehā, sometimes keeping a distance from that word. A name is needed that honours the culture they brought with them to Aotearoa and the commitment they've made to live here under the common protection and embrace of the treaty.

Krishna Pillai expresses the need for a name that speaks of belonging here when you are neither Māori nor traditionally European. 'I am a product of the British Empire, I am a mixture of displaced Irish, middle class English, eloping Indian, indentured labour and Commonwealth funds.' He describes himself like this: 'I am a mongrel, a blend, a melange, I am a Kiwi. A person who has no other home. A person who loves the sparkling waters, the dripping rainforests and playful piwakawaka ... A person for whom boarding the Air New Zealand waka to be greeted by flattened vowels, well-rounded and healthy-looking cabin crew and recorded kōkako call on the way home from a rite-of-passage OE was thrilling, emotional and relieving all at once.' And yet, he points out, 'No matter how much I listen to Dunedin Sound, wear gumboots to the supermarket or how much I swim in frozen rivers, lakes and seas, I am encouraged to tick the box "Indian". And if I don't then others will do it for me as I discovered in this new age of access to your own health records. Or they might even tick the box Fijian as that is where my father was born.'

Although this dissonance has defined his life, 'It has probably made me the person I am now. Growing up in white 1970s Dunedin I was definitely unusual and that may have afforded me advantages as well. I guess in those days I was not Māori so that was in my favour. Of course now the tables have turned. As most New Zealanders I meet now, I honour and treasure all things Māori. I aspire to matauranga Māori and am excited by my nascent te reo. But no matter how much I do these things I have no whakapapa.'

One possibility for these New Zealanders who are not of, or not entirely of, European descent might be to employ the name given to this country in the treaty itself – Niu Tireni. So alongside Pākehā there would be Niu Tireni Indian, Niu Tireni Vietnamese. In the last decade another alternative has emerged, one that Māori increasingly welcome and advocate. As partners to the tangata whenua, the people of the land, everyone else who is not Māori, regardless of where they came from, is tangata tiriti, the people of the treaty. (Krishna Pillai is happy with this name.) This is, however, no less demanding – you are acknowledging the treaty as your right to be here – but it does avoid making people of European descent a privileged category of Kiwi.

Debbie Ngarewa-Packer, co-leader of the Māori Party, is an eloquent advocate for this naming. 'Tangata tiriti are people who don't argue about the existence of Te Tiriti o Waitangi as our founding document ... They are secure in themselves and know we are equals' and they believe that 'our combined whakapapa is the rongoa (remedy) for the future'. She also points out that tangata tiriti understand that the treaty 'didn't create special rights for Māori – we already had Māori social structures and systems of lore in place. Te Tiriti was put in place to provide for Pākehā, because the settlers migrating to Aotearoa didn't fall under British law.' So perhaps we can expect to see tangata tiriti used more frequently. It makes the basis for belonging crystal clear. But it also describes Māori, not by their belonging but by their relationship with Pākehā. What it doesn't do is say much about their culture as colonial settler and now post-colonial Pākehā.

Of course there are some who prefer to avoid any label; to simply call themselves New Zealanders and wait for this bicultural wave to wash past. But the chances of that happening aren't good.

* * *

The cultural context of what it means to be Pākehā will continue to expand to reflect the complications it embraces. And it's a rich culture, bound up in memories and places – whether roadmen's sheds, school bus shelters, old cream stands – that are worth taking stock of, for they are richer and more important than Pākehā imagine. As I wrote once in a poem, they are 'like an old address book' in the heads of Pākehā like me, not missed 'until they reconnect, clack, clunk/like railway carriage couplings/that carry me into new complexities'. They can mark out 'the pathway of a heritage/I walk, knowing where to put my feet'.

Food is another powerful ingredient of Pākehā identity, shared, of course, with Māori but shaped initially by northern hemisphere traditions and evolving into Kiwi patterns. The instinct to feed people, even when they're not hungry, is buried in the Kiwi DNA, and it began with Māori, whose overwhelming and surprising generosity kept Pākehā from starving. Then, to fight homesickness and loneliness, came scones and cups of tea to entertain friends and strangers, and, later, the *Edmonds Cookery Book*, the Holy Book of feeding each other properly. And ever since, Pākehā New Zealanders have been bringing a plate and pot lucking. Even today, in these more sophisticated times, it's hard to beat the welcome of sponge cakes stuck together with jam, asparagus (tinned is best) in white bread rolls, Anzac biscuits and Afghans, ginger crunch (found in smart cafés everywhere) or gems and, beloved by the adults at children's birthday parties, buttered white bread with hundreds and thousands. But even as the Kiwi code of hospitality and the menus keep expanding, care and effort, respect for others, sharing food at a table remain paramount. In hospitality given or received, Māori and Pākehā can see each other with fresh eyes, make room for new people.

And then there's the geography of the country. Living in a 'long place', as Maurice Andrew once called it, with a temperate climate, to say nothing of being free from snakes and scorpions, has its effect on who we think we are. Māori share that, obviously, but they had a 700-year head start in adapting to it and shaping their culture accordingly.

At a meeting I attended at Ōhinemutu, after days of difficult debate about sharing money and resources with Māori, and lots of fractured relationships as a result, members of both cultures sat down to dinner. A band struck up and a vocalist stood up and started to move between the tables singing 'Won't you come home, Bill Bailey, won't you come home'. The music had an electrifying effect on everyone and the tone of the conversation that night suddenly shifted, thanks to an imported song. It didn't rely on everyone agreeing but spoke to the humanity we shared and sparked a new desire to listen to each other. The music that neither culture could claim as their own had reframed everyone, both Māori and Pākehā.

Spiritually and culturally Pākehā still have a way to go, but the political content of their identity will become much sharper, as the treaty reference grows more focused. Teacher Tamsin Hanly, who has written and published six books called *A Critical Guide to Māori and Pākehā Histories,* argues that to name our culture as Pākehā is to decentre it and reposition it as an 'other' culture, not necessarily normal or needing to be dominant.

That can be very helpful when you're trying to describe where we belong. Sir Paul Reeves grew up as a Pākehā but much later in life claimed his Māori ancestry and identified as Māori, playing a leading role in his Taranaki iwi. When I asked him why, he replied that Māori always have to make a choice. 'Pākehā can live happily in their non-Māori world, oblivious to anything Māori. But Māori have to live in both.' Pākehā never describe themselves as part Pākehā, but we talk glibly of people who are part Māori, as if it's an identity you can slip off like a coat when it gets too hot. Māori know it's permanent clothing that you need to wear to keep yourself proud.

There are other terms to consider, of course. Tangata tiriti is a bit juridical and formal for some. Tauiwi has the feel of distance and otherness about it. It can mean foreign, even alien. Manuhiri also: do Pākehā always want to be known as the visitors? Non-Māori? Who wants to define themselves by what they're not rather than what they are? And let's not overload Pākehā with more precision than it can carry. Making it interchangeable with the Crown doesn't work either, because the government belongs as much to Māori as it does to Pākehā. I think we're stuck with Pākehā. It's as much about relationship as it is about identity. It's a word used nowhere else in the world, about no one else.

* * *

Women come at this business of self-identity differently. Alison Jones does so vividly in *This Pākehā Life*. The female version of this story needs to stand alongside the male; women are no less accountable about the colonial history all Pākehā share. The 1993 Suffrage Day service in Christchurch took place at a time when sexual abuse within and outside my own church was being confronted. I was part of a group that tried to have a plaque inside the cathedral, which would have read: 'As bishops, male clergy and laity of the Diocese of Christchurch, we condemn the violence and other abuse against women in our church, our community and our own lives. Together as men we repent for our actions and our silence. We seek a future where women and men can laugh and cry and trust and dream together.' We tried to say this as Pākehā men, not speaking for Māori, though we knew Māori clergy were struggling to address the same issues. But the plaque was never publicly erected, quickly branded by Pākehā men as divisive, defensive, overstated and unnecessary. Would it have succeeded had it been a bicultural initiative?

So much of the work on Pākehā identity has been framed in male terms, as Jock Phillips' significant work, *A Man's Country?*, made clear. Men of my era, especially those whose understanding of women was formed in the dormitories of boys' boarding schools, have had to be reconstructed and we're still a work in progress. My wife has had to make that a lifelong task, and I've been helped, nudged and sometimes booted along by women parishioners, students and staff colleagues wherever I've worked. I've had to not only watch my language but also to rewrite it, and to know when to stand back and shut up. I'm learning, but not well enough yet, because I'm surrounded by old, white men like myself who find this bicultural debate deeply troubling. I want to say to them: remember we had to reinvent ourselves to be able to work and live respectfully and happily with women, to trust and be trusted by them. Maybe Pākehā have to go through something similar with Māori.

CHAPTER 16

Do Pākehā need protocols?

There is kawa, a set of protocols and etiquette, to guide behaviour in both Māori and Pākehā cultures. But, as with so many other bicultural issues, Kiwis seem to be very aware of how special and different Māori kawa is, and unaware that a Pākehā equivalent even exists. And, if it does, they consider that it's no more than behaving normally. There is, naturally, common ground, kawa that both cultures have to follow to survive, like driving on the left-hand side of the road. There's one road code for all, but how it's enforced became contentious during the Covid-19 pandemic, with iwi-initiated roadblocks checking up on motorists entering their areas. And the public hospital system used to have standard protocols for all patients until health boards learnt to make special rules for Māori concerning visitor access, consultation with whānau, and protocols surrounding death and dying.

The common ground where one size fits all is narrowing by the day. Kawa is rapidly becoming a two-track affair. Consider the Māori Party's successful challenge to the parliamentary dress code, which ended in ties no longer being mandatory and hats being permitted. Māori kawa is very clear to any Pākehā who bothers to check out the local marae. Giving and receiving the hongi, taking your shoes off, not sitting on tables or pillows became familiar behaviour in the 1970s. In 1986 Hiwi and Patricia Tauroa wrote a bestseller about it – *Te Marae: A Guide to Customs and Protocols.*

But the list is much longer now and more complex, even though it's always been there, hidden from Pākehā eyes: respecting personal space, looking at the person you're talking to, not walking in front of a speaker, but waiting or crouching down to show respect as you pass, not stepping over people seated on the ground (especially not women over men), keeping not only bottoms but also hats and bags away from surfaces where food is or will be placed, not touching someone's head, and not passing food overhead. It's a long list, all to do with respecting a person's mana or status and the distinction between what is tapu and noa, ordinary and sacred. Some of the constraints make instant sense and should be shared easily, cross-culturally, such as not spitting and not yelling at waiters but waiting to make eye contact. Others are subtle and learnt only by engaging with Māori day by day.

But what about Pākehā kawa? Beyond shaking hands, is there such a thing? Our forebears arriving from Europe were very clear that there was, in a transplanted form from the old country. It was a highly structured way of behaving properly, at first defined by social class but quickly adapted as settlers rewrote the rules that we still laugh at in such programmes as *Downton*

Abbey. The so-called lower classes delighted in upsetting protocol. Workmen when they got to New Zealand saw themselves as good as their masters. Servant girls refused to stand when talking to their mistresses and words like 'servant' and 'maid' faded from the colonial vocabulary. To be 'up yourself' became a major offence in the Pākehā code. It became acceptable to drop in on neighbours unannounced, as rural people still do, and it was polite to offer visiting tradies a cup of morning tea, and rude for them to refuse. Women were the guardians of Pākehā kawa, making sure men understood the importance of standing when a woman entered a room and opening doors for her; then, with the feminist revolution, regarding these behaviours as patronising, chauvinist and reinforcing of inequality.

In the laid-back, anti-authoritarian 2000s where informality is the new standard, kawa may seem to have disappeared, but it's simply changed its spots. It's culturally acceptable now to wear pretty much anything you like (though it's preferable you wear something) when going out in public, but it needs to be clean and you're expected to present yourself thoughtfully, even to the deliberate rip in your jeans or the cultivated disarray of your hairstyle. And if it's dinner, you need to bring something, like a bottle of wine or kombucha. If it's the pub with friends, then don't leave before buying your round. (They tried to ban that habit officially during the First World War but it didn't work.) Much Pākehā kawa is still focused on children's behaviour: learning to say please and thank you, asking to leave the table, not eating before everyone's ready, not speaking over grown-ups (though that one is rapidly fading). In the *Little Red School Book*, children were urged to 'Demand your rights, but be polite'. Would that make it into today's edition with Greta Thunberg demanding that young people yell their defiance at the stupidity and greed of their climate-heating elders?

The flash point for Pākehā kawa is focused on cell phones and the use of electronic devices. On Facebook and Twitter all the old conventions of decency, courtesy and restraint have been abandoned, replaced by a feral, manic, conspiracy-driven culture that refuses to heed any effective regulation. With that toxic and terrifying dark underground just a thumb press away, it's all the more important to preserve some measure of decency and mutual respect in the daylight world. That's what kawa, both Pākehā and Māori, tries to do. And happily there's a new kawa emerging, shared by both cultures, regarding digitally driven behaviour. Don't talk loudly on your phone in public spaces. Don't use your phone while eating or in a meeting or talking to a shop assistant or anyone else for that matter, and certainly not for long. There's no polite way to say in the midst of an important conversation, in any culture, 'I've got to take this.'

Kawa includes what we wear. Māori dress styles have long been thoroughly Europeanised, but commonly with a distinctive twist or special flair – a pendant or earring often of pounamu, a design feature such as a koru. Pākehā do some, but only some, of that. Some Māori wear their iwi name on their sleeve or their T-shirt. Pākehā more often wear the name of their rugby team.

And fewer and fewer events and rituals distinctive to Pākehā aren't shared with Māori. A&P shows (axe chopping aside), sailing regattas (I didn't see South Auckland get too excited about winning the America's Cup), cricket matches (Ross Taylor notwithstanding) and exotic sports like polo and lacrosse, bridge but not golf have all been largely Pākehā. But that's shifting now. Matariki, now an official public holiday, is competing with Christmas and Easter and supplanting Guy Fawkes; Waitangi Day means more to New Zealanders than Queen's Birthday or Labour Day. Anzac Day endures as an important shared ritual. Kapa haka and waka ama competitions remain largely Māori events, as do the annual Rātana birthday events, except for the day the politicians visit, and the two cultures still tend to mourn separately, but much else of what they do is governed by a blend of kawa.

As is the Kiwi sense of humour. I think there are some cultural differences there, though Pākehā laughed as readily as Māori at Billy T. James' jokes and some Māori friends tell me they thought Fred Dagg was funny too. In Pakiri my Māori neighbours and I say things to each other that I'd never dare to print. One of them invokes his treaty rights to criticise how I mow my lawns and where he's allowed to park his car and I'm not. If he wasn't a good friend, I would be treading carefully in how I responded.

To be able to laugh together about the same thing requires being comfortable about enjoying the same space and the same way of seeing the world, if only for a moment. Sometimes Pākehā can find that's possible with Māori and vice versa. But is there something especially Pākehā droll about this item on Radio New Zealand in which a police officer was being interviewed about a bomb discovered in a car boot in Kaikohe?

'Was it timed to go off at a precise time?' asked the interviewer.

'Maybe,' said the officer, 'but the precise time hasn't come yet.' Then he paused for a moment, before adding, 'And we'd have known if it had because we were standing next to it.'

I think that's quintessentially Pākehā, with a nod to British roots – the sort of humour that marks the anecdote about the woman who, having just heard the BBC announcement in 1939 that war had been declared, turned to her husband and said, 'Oh well, dear, I'll put the kettle on and we'll have a nice cup of tea.'

Historian Erik Olssen has written about that ingredient of humour in Pākehā kawa in reflecting on the way meeting styles have changed in the academic world and observed in a Māori friend. 'Much of it centres on the frivolity, the refusal to accept things, especially those things that are portrayed as serious and important, at face value ... Teasing – usually of a gentle nature – was also a source of endless amusement and easily turned into banter.' In meetings of the committee they sat on, Olssen realised that although much of the humour 'involved questions of mana, individual, family or even tribal ... it was also a style that permeated all activities and denied any pretence, called in question all sacred things, almost as if in mocking the sacred itself mana might change hands.'

By contrast, the difference between cultures is stark in the tone Māori and Pākehā use to talk to and about each other. That tone has become embedded in our respective kawa, for better and, currently, for worse, if the present state of acrimonious debate is anything to go by. Tone is what makes or breaks our willingness to listen to music. If the singer is flat, or the orchestra out of tune, we quickly give up. We find it insulting, excruciatingly hard to hear and we judge performers incompetent. The same can happen with the way we speak to each other.

Time and again during the Covid-19 pandemic, Māori and Pasifika communities complained bitterly about being patronised and blamed for messaging sent through channels they didn't trust and in vocabularies they didn't understand. A spokesperson for the Samoan Assembly of God church in Mangere, the scene of a superspreader event, said their experience of health officials speaking to them was 'denting, demanding and blaming'. But when Pasifika providers were called in to do the testing, unlike the earlier record of no shows, 750 showed up to be tested, even though there were only 500 in the congregation. There's nothing new about any of this. A Māori delegate at an Anglican synod meeting back in 1876, when asked why he walked out, replied, 'What's the use of going when you have to stand there like a post? Don't they know Māori have minds and tongues of their own?'

Pākehā can be quick to judge victims of poverty and dispossession, to blame them for not helping themselves, to grumble when they don't understand Māori while expecting them to comprehend every word they speak. Pākehā have built a Kiwi culture of complaint over generations, then wonder why Māori adopt it as well. There's a deep vein of Puritanism running through the Pākehā bloodstream, inherited from Calvinist, evangelical and fundamentalist Protestant and Catholic missionaries, that made pleasure, especially of a sexual kind, into an instant sin; driven by theologies obsessed with what's wrong rather than what's right about humanity. And if you wonder whether that Pākehā legacy is still alive and well, try reading the letters to the editor page in any New Zealand newspaper.

To make it worse, some Pākehā seem ready to transfer that grumbling dissatisfaction onto Māori, accusing them of ingratitude for all the good things that have been done for them. That transference was very visible in Garrick Tremain's cartoons, such as the one in the *Otago Daily Times* of 31 August 2000, showing a group of chiefs watching the arrival of the first European sailing ships. 'At last!' says one. 'Somebody to blame!' As journalist Joel Maxwell puts it, 'the working rule of racism is that whatever racists are currently moaning about is the opposite of the truth.'

The bicultural future we're struggling to find will require a different tone from some Pākehā – more respectful, a little less grim, a lot more willing to live with ambiguity and uncertainty, because the identity they're seeking is still a work in progress. Being tentative is okay in this new future, as is a lighter, less earnest, funnier tone.

CHAPTER 17

Promises, promises

Sitting at the heart of this search for a bicultural future is a document that won't go away, despite our best efforts to lose it. It's been locked up and neglected, damaged by water and eaten by rats; its multiple copies have been scattered and altered; its Māori version has been endlessly disputed and mistranslated. It's been declared null and void. Māori have never lost sight of it. Many Pākehā have preferred to forget it.

Very soon after the Treaty of Waitangi/Te Tiriti o Waitangi was signed on 6 February 1840, tensions emerged over how well it would be honoured. In the early years, the Crown, in the form of the British Colonial Office, government agents and successive governors, gave reassurances. A protector of aborigines was created two months after the signing but the office was abolished in 1846. A year later Queen Victoria sent assurances, in response to a petition from Tainui chief Te Wherowhero, that the treaty would be honoured. That didn't happen. In the face of expanding European settlement and greed for land, iwi drew strength from numbers and unity. In

Waikato, a federation of Tainui tribes, which also involved iwi outside the rohe, developed into the Māori King Movement, Te Kīngitanga. In 1858 Te Wherowhero was crowned as the first Māori king, Pōtatau. The Māori of the Kīngitanga saw this establishment of a monarch similar in status to the British queen, and existing in peace beside her, as a means of retaining their land. The government saw it as treason and Governor George Grey's invasion of Waikato marked the beginning of warfare that eroded what little trust remained.

The anti-treaty lobbying had long been intense. In 1844 the New Zealand Company, intent on buying up land for new settlers, told a select committee in the British House of Commons that the treaty was little more than a 'praiseworthy device for amusing and pacifying savages for the moment'. A change in the British government caused a change in attitude. By 1847 a new colonial secretary was promoting Crown control over any land that was unoccupied or uncultivated, and a decade later the Colonial Office had done little to restrain the settlers, who had been given almost completely free rein. The new colonial parliament, established in 1854, did little to help, sharing none of its power with Māori.

The treaty had guaranteed the Crown pre-emption of land as a way of controlling sales and safeguarding Māori rights, but after war began in Taranaki in 1860, and later in Waikato, the Native Lands Act of 1862 got rid of this. The treaty seemed a long time ago. It would be another 113 years before it was once again incorporated into the law of the land.

Ambiguous court judgements on the treaty didn't help. Rather than seeing the treaty as the source of land rights, in an 1847 case the first Chief Justice William Martin and Justice Henry Chapman (as a staunch New Zealand Company supporter) used common law thinking derived from the United States to deliberately narrow the treaty's scope. The thinking was based on the 'doctrine of discovery', which had long been used to legitimise the taking of indigenous people's land. It allowed colonisers to decide what, if any, rights 'natives' might have left to them after Europeans had 'discovered', in other words invaded, their lands.

Despite all the difficulties and differences of opinion surrounding the treaty, Māori remained dominant in New Zealand, at least until they were outnumbered by Pākehā in 1859. Then the balance shifted dramatically: by 1861 there were 100,000 Pākehā to 60,000 Māori. Before that, however, in the words of James Belich, 'as far as most Māori were concerned, British empire over them was false'. In the day to day, beyond the main settlements, Pākehā law had limited grip and tended to work 'only when Māori let it'. Under the limited protection of the treaty, the Māori economy flourished through the 1840s and 1850s right up to the outbreak of war. Their farms, gardens, orchards and flour mills fed Pākehā settlers; their trading vessels plied the Tasman. In 1863 women and children were burned and killed at the Waikato settlement of Rangiaowhia in a battle with British troops, but when Austrian geologist Ferdinand von Hochstetter visited only four years before, he found flourishing

wheat, maize and potato fields, roads, horses and healthy cattle –
even a racecourse and a courthouse, as well as both Catholic and
Protestant churches.

It took Pākehā another century to rediscover and revalue the
promises made in the treaty and to stop trying to get rid of it, or
overlook it, or pretend it didn't really apply to them. And some
are still trying. Some political commentators have argued that,
rather than being a democratic document, the treaty resembles a
deal done between a group of chiefs in New Zealand and a super
chief, Queen Victoria, on the other side of the world. Others claim
it's an arrangement with the Crown, not the rest of us; still others
argue that what it meant in 1840 is quite different to the claims
made about it today. The evasions go on and on. Conversations
about the Treaty of Waitangi/Te Tiriti o Waitangi are full of
people talking past each other, even down to what it should be
called. To use the Māori name implies you start with the Māori
text and understand the guarantee it offers of tino rangatiratanga.

But implication isn't enough if both partners are to honour
this treaty. Something more than legalities and verbal translations
is needed. In 1975 the Treaty of Waitangi Act was the first of
a wave of new legislation that began to weave treaty references
into law, protecting Māori land, upholding fishing rights, setting
up the Waitangi Tribunal, which could address both recent
Māori land claims and later those dating back to 1840, and
requiring state-owned enterprises to address treaty claims. In
1987 the President of the Court of Appeal, Justice Robin Cooke,
revalidated the treaty as 'compact of mutual obligation' and a

year later the Royal Commission on Social Policy called for it to be 'entrenched as a constitutional document'. In 2000 Sir Paul Reeves chaired a national conference at Parliament buildings that explored how to do that. Most mainstream churches were strongly supportive, but that momentum ebbed away, lost in the furore over foreshore and seabed legislation, the Global Financial Crisis, earthquakes and massacres.

Pākehā perception of the treaty remains easily distracted; even insisting on referring to it by its Māori name doesn't always improve their focus. It makes the Māori understanding clearer but can have the effect of accelerating Pākehā avoidance. And there's plenty of that. Mitzi Nairn of the ecumenical Programme on Racism had a list of signposts to show how Pākehā have avoided engaging with the treaty. One is just to walk away, as the Pākehā MPs did in the 1890s when the Kotahitanga MPs introduced new legislation that would honour the treaty. They simply left the House so a quorum couldn't be formed.

Another is to rearrange the words of treaty promises, as happened with Bastion Point. By 1855, Ngāti Whatua had lost title to all their lands except the 700-acre (280-hectare) Ōrākei Block. This was officially declared inalienable in 1869, but only 13 individual owners were appointed. In 1951 the Crown compulsorily acquired the last 12.5 acres (5 hectares) of the block, leaving the hapū landless, with the exception of the quarter-acre (1000-square-metre) cemetery.

And perhaps the most powerful avoidance of all on Mitzi's list is the tactic of retelling stories of treaty promises to make villains out of the victims. She often told the story of Hōne Heke, the Ngāpuhi chief who was first to sign the treaty, chopping down the flagpole at Kororāreka (later Russell) in 1844. Pākehā history has portrayed that as an act of violent aggression against the Crown. No mention of the fact that he owned the flagpole and had erected it to fly the flag of the United Tribes *of New Zealand,* a confederation of Māori tribes based in the Far North. Once the treaty was signed, the flagpole was used to fly the Union Jack, much to Heke's displeasure. He saw the treaty being dishonoured and wrote to the governor, 'I cut down the flagpole, firstly because it was mine, and secondly because it had neither breath nor bones/blood and could feel no pain.'

* * *

Legally and constitutionally the treaty isn't going to go away. The legal mindset that measures its validity only by the number of times it is incorporated into legislation is beginning to shift. It is slowly being regarded as something to be respected in its own right as our nation's founding document, our own Magna Carta. But it won't come closer in Pākehā consciousness until it is seen in the spirit in which it was conceived and signed. Drafted, translated and promoted with the help of missionaries and the mission-educated chiefs who helped them to craft the written language it relied on, spread and interpreted around the country to the more than 500 chiefs who signed it, the treaty in its original context was as much a spiritual as a legal document.

That was partly because of the style of Māori used by Henry Williams and his son Edward when they were asked to translate the draft of the treaty, overnight, on 4 February 1840, ready for discussion with the chiefs the next day. Gaining their agreement was crucial, and the translation was the key: the words used must be familiar. Father and son, with advice from the chiefs, therefore relied on vocabulary used in Māori translations of biblical texts, which had been appearing since the 1820s and had been widely disseminated throughout the 1830s by mission-educated Māori catechists, teachers and chiefs. The two words on which the treaty was to pivot came from those sources: rangatiratanga or kingly rule, as in 'thy kingdom come', is from the Lord's Prayer; kāwanatanga or governorship is from the appointment of Roman governor Pontius Pilate, who managed affairs in Jerusalem but was careful not to trespass on the authority of the Jewish king, Herod. The chiefs who would be gathering to discuss the treaty knew exactly what these words meant. The formula was clear – a balance between governorship given to the British queen and final authority retained by the chiefs, nothing less than the 'full exclusive and undisturbed possession of their lands and estates, forests, fisheries and other properties'.

It's understanding the nature of that authority retained by the chiefs that has caused so much grief for Māori and so much confusion for Pākehā minds ever since. Māori never for a moment thought they were giving it away. No chief in his right mind would consider surrendering the very mana that entitled him to be signing the treaty in the first place. Rangatiratanga, the word the chiefs helped Williams and his son to choose, described the highest kind of authority, but the word was strengthened with an addition: te tino rangatiratanga – not simply authority but true or absolute authority. For them this was a solemn and sacred covenant. Other elements in the treaty subject to that same covenantal understanding, the understanding of Māori lore, for example, as it applied to land ownership, to be protected as 'rights and privileges' that Māori would enjoy in the same way as British subjects enjoyed their own. That protection quickly evaporated and the concept of a gift given in trust, with the giver retaining an interest and a benefit, led to endless anger and bloodshed.

* * *

There's no legal doubt about the authority of those two words, kāwanatanga and rangatiratanga, in the Māori text of the treaty. The United Nations has said that any treaty between an incoming colonial interest and the indigenous community is to be understood in terms of the indigenous language version, and so it won't do to say, 'Oh, but the English translation isn't as strong.' And if the legal meaning is clear, the spiritual covenant that envelops them is even more so. Māori understood covenant more clearly than Governor Hobson and his officers. The word has a very particular meaning in Christian vocabulary. It evokes the story of of Moses leading his people to a Promised Land and the story of the Last Supper, where Jesus makes a blood and flesh, wine and bread compact with his followers. Māori very deliberately applied that same biblical word to the treaty. Ngāpuhi rangatira Hōne Heke and Eruera Maihi Patuone both likened the treaty to a covenant, as did missionary John Hobbs and the chiefs at the Mangungu signing, and the chiefs who attended the Kohimarama Conference held in 1860 in an attempt to prevent the fighting in Taranaki from spreading further. It's easy to understand why Māori were so outraged when the treaty was broken and when missionaries were seen to betray them by taking the side of the settlers.

* * *

A spiritual defining of the treaty was nothing unusual in the Māori world. Matauranga (knowledge) was all about the co-existence of seen and unseen, the physical and the spiritual beyond human grasp; and the balance, reciprocity and equilibrium between these different realities. And weaving all that together were whakapapa links, kinship networks that bound people to one another in the natural and the supernatural worlds. Buddhist, Muslim and Hindu traditions are equally rich in awareness of realities beyond the physical and rational, but Pākehā can struggle to get their heads around all that, not least because their own heritage of spirituality has often become so disconnected, dispersed and devalued. Although they have deep spiritual roots to draw on in Jewish and Christian heritages, much of that has been neglected in a secular, consumer-driven society.

For many Pākehā, spiritual discernment – being able to recognise the hidden, unspoken, largely unseen value and beauty of places and things, even documents like the Treaty of Waitangi – has become a lost art. It's very hard to put it into words. One term some writers and poets use is thin places, where the veil between what is secular and sacred, ordinary and extraordinary is easier to see through than thick places where your eyes don't penetrate the concrete and the stone. Another word is liminal, as in crossing over point, walking through the door or window framed by a lintel beam, and moving from one realm of being to another.

Some places are thinner, more liminal than others. Beaches, gardens, bush-clad hills, of course, but some buildings too. Movie theatres rate pretty high on my list – old ones, like the Civic in Auckland, and the Latter-day Saints hall used for movies in Nūhaka, though Heritage New Zealand wasn't interested in saving that one. Thin places and thin documents. Te Tiriti o Waitangi would become thin for us if we could learn to see it as Māori do – and that isn't as it was in 1840 because it has taken on a life of its own, through its long journey of neglect and betrayal, hard-won revival and gradual honouring.

In a poem about the 1940 festivities that marked 100 years since the signing of the treaty, Denis Glover wrote that among the 'centennial splendours' – the fireworks, the decorated cars, the ponga-draped verandahs, the politicians' platitudes – 'no one remembered our failures'. We've got a couple of decades to go before 2040, the date which that thorny document, *He Puapua*, invites us to envision. I'm wondering if anyone will need to read Glover's poem again, then. Part of the answer will depend on the willingness of Pākehā to entertain a less materialist way of seeing the world, with a touch more sympathy for the things that connect us not only mind and heart but also body and soul.

In the Rodney region where I live there is a flood of new business ventures promoting spirituality through massage, retreat and meditation in lovely garden settings, organic products, skin cleansing, therapies and diets. None of the advertised remedies have any treaty-based reference or invoke partnership with Māori in their advertising, though the opportunity is there with traditional medicine, indigenous healing rituals and natural products. Pākehā know something about spirituality when it's a health and leisure pursuit, a therapeutic alternative, but the treaty requires us to see spirituality as a political invitation as well, a way of helping them to honour promises their forebears made so they can live here proudly now, as keepers of a covenant.

CHAPTER 18

Would you drive a hybrid?

It's bad enough to confiscate a people's land, or force them to sell it by changing the title, to outlaw their spirituality or to ban their language in schools, but passing laws that say who is allowed to call themselves Māori takes racism to a whole other level. The history of legislation that tries to define a Māori looks like a game of snakes and ladders. In the beginning everyone in Aotearoa was Māori, though more often they would describe themselves by hapū and whakapapa links. In English they were known as aboriginals and, most commonly, New Zealanders, at a time when settlers still called themselves British. Included in *A Grammar and Vocabulary of the Language of New Zealand*, published in 1820, was the question 'Ka Māori tia te pākehā?' – 'Have the Pākehā become ordinary/one of us?' As Alison Jones and Kuni Kaa Jenkins suggest, it also meant 'Will they adjust to ordinary life and ideas? Or will they try to remain different, standing apart?'

In the early colonial period, at least until Pākehā become the majority in the 1860s, there was no need to try to define who

Māori were, and early Pākehā were more interested in fitting in than standing apart. But as the pressure to acquire land grew, through legal and illegal means, war and confiscation, so did the pressure on deciding who could claim to be Māori. The 1877 Census Act shifted them into categories that were not to be counted as Māori, if, for example, they decided to 'live as Pākehā' in wooden houses. That continued to apply until 1936, when the registrar-general of the day declared that 'the blending of the races had largely been achieved'. That sentiment continued and confirmed in official documents, up until as late as 1980 by the Human Rights Commission.

But social attitudes as much as legal definitions shaped how people identified as Māori. In the first 40 years of Pākehā settlement, interracial marriage was widespread. (Unlike in the United States, such unions were never legally banned.) Many children of early missionaries did so, and later British soldiers, though mistresses seemed to be more common than wives. A letter to the editor of Auckland's *Daily Southern Cross* in 1848 drew attention to the growing problem of mixed-race children – or 'this Anglo-maori race', as the writer described them – 'there are at least five hundred children in these islands growing up to call the white man father', who was likely to desert them 'from penury, death, or indifference'. These children would also face difficulties in ever acquiring title to land. Pākehā men were applauded for taking Māori wives because it would 'civilise' these women, whereas if a Pākehā woman married a Māori man she would be 'going native'. From the 1860s interracial marriage became less popular for Pākehā men who faced the accusation of being motivated by land grabbing. Angela Wanhalla's *Matters of the Heart*, which looks at the history of interracial marriage in New Zealand, provides a fascinating survey of these attitudes and of theories about miscegenation, which she describes as 'the pseudo-scientific study of racial crossings'.

The interest in this, and in eugenics, which attempted to ensure the reproduction of only desirable heritable characteristics, led to such appalling legislation as the Chinese Immigrants Act of 1881, which imposed a £10 poll tax on all Chinese arrivals in New Zealand. But awareness of the subject was not confined to Pākehā. In 1928 Āpirana Ngata spoke of the need to study and explain 'the brown tinge in the future New Zealander' and soon after set up a commission of inquiry in response to public unease about the status of Māori women working in Asian-run market gardens. Its report felt that 'indiscriminate intermingling of the lower types of races – i.e. Māoris, Chinese and Hindus' would eventually lead to the deterioration of both Māori 'and the national life of this country', by creating 'a hybrid race'. Te Rangi Hiroa (Sir Peter Buck) welcomed mixed marriages and racial blending: 'It is an inevitable process which has taken place down the ages and the blending of the two races into New Zealand citizenship should do away ultimately with the bickering between pākehā and Māori.'

Social attitudes and legal changes played tag with each other for a century or so. In the words of legal scholar Dr David Williams, New Zealand's statute book is 'full to overflowing with various definitions based on race categories such "aboriginal", "native", "Māori", "European", "Chinese", "Asiatic", etc.' As he points out, the definition given in the Māori Welfare Act 'was the first move away from the half-caste terminology': it stated that '"Māori" means a person belonging to the aboriginal race of New Zealand; and includes any descendant of a Māori.'. The most recent legal definition, in the Te Ture Whenua Māori Act 1993, is 'a person of the Māori race of New Zealand; and includes any descendant of a Māori'. And so finally, whakapapa rather than fraction of blood quotient becomes the criterion, thus ending a century of percentage guessing and the most bizarre criteria for racial redesign. Take the Native Laws Amendment Act of 1912, for example. By application to the Native Land Court, Māori could apply to be 'Europeanised' – the governor would 'declare a native to be European' – provided they were 'acquainted with the English language', possessed the required educational qualifications, had sufficient land or was able to earn enough 'by reason of some special profession, trade, or calling'.

And were Māori holding their breath for someone to tell them who they could become, let alone who they were? For all those who were watching Pākehā-led institutions decide whether Māori could or couldn't be who they were, the farce was over. It would have made a good Gilbert and Sullivan operetta if it wasn't so tragic. By the end of the twentieth century, half of all Māori men were living in a relationship with partners who were not Māori.

* * *

Common ground shared equally by Māori and Pākehā is tough territory to live in. When institutions attempt it, there are constant questions about motive, balance, equity, agenda setting, resource sharing and a fear that the merging will dissolve and devalue difference. The Anglicans tried to make it work with Common Life Hui in the first years of their three-tikanga constitution, but they gradually faded away. Pākehā didn't persist and many Māori said they had more pressing issues in ordering their own affairs.

Anxiety about the loss of control over copyright is another theme in finding common ground. Who gives Air New Zealand the right to put koru patterns on its plane tails? What does Lorde think she's doing singing in te reo and weaving Māori images into her music videos? Who gives her the right as a Pākehā, even if she's famous, to say, 'I'm not Māori, but all New Zealanders grow up with elements of this world view. Te ao Māori and tikanga Māori are a big part of why people who aren't from here intuit our country to be kind of "magical".'

Lorde's Māori critics accused her of tokenism; some argued her album triggered language loss trauma. Otago University senior lecturer and columnist Morgan Godfery (Te Pahipoto, Samoa) defended her: 'If we must wait for perfect circumstances to speak or sing te reo rangatira … we may as well sign the language's death certificate … [For] the language to survive it must act as a functional language, deployed across institutions, mediums and communities both Māori and non-Māori.'

And what about those graphics that opened TV coverage of the last America's Cup? A striking blend of Māori and Pākehā images that slipped across our screens in a digital dance, it was a daily prelude to a broadcast panel of hosts from both cultures.

Even more vexed is the debate about what's essential in our respective cultures. Pākehā, with their polyglot and haphazard origins, often don't know where to start that conversation, but the Māori search for essentialism is taken much more seriously. Before the artworks that formed the *Te Māori* exhibition departed for their New York showing in 1984, small chips were taken from some of the carvings to preserve their essence in case they accidentally disappeared. Imagine Pākehā attempting such an insurance of their treasures. How would they ever know where to begin, let alone agree on what was essential to preserve. Pākehā culture is shaped by multiple heritages, some recent arrivals, still in the process of being melded and bedded down in the landscape. Māori have a thousand-year head start in finding that clarity and focus.

There's an element of romance in the quest for what's essential and pure in both cultures. I wouldn't begin to attempt that analysis for Māori, but in my Pākehā world, utopian and arcadian longings are easy to see. Take the way the country is packaged for overseas tourists – clean, green and pure, a land of sublime images, crossed by lakes and rivers no one would never dream of polluting, bush they'd never dare to fell and burn, animals they wouldn't kill and eat, whose brains they'd never think of marketing as sweetbreads. Pākehā have romanticised themselves shamelessly to attract visitors, wrapping it all in myths about giving everyone a fair go.

* * *

Like it or not, hybridity is here to stay in Aotearoa. Since the beginning of Pākehā settlement it's always been about entanglement, right from the arrival of the missionaries, who led the way in weaving the two cultures together through, as historian Tony Ballantyne says, 'work and trade, prayer and worship, travel and commensality [eating together], conversation and argument, and mutual concern in times of illness and death'. And mission stations weren't separate 'little Englands'. Unlike the violence that would come three decades later, leaving consequences with which all New Zealanders still live, this wasn't about trying to destroy Māori culture but changing it through 'translation, conversation and debate'. And the two cultures also connected through the exchange of gifts between friends: Samuel Marsden gave Ruatara seeds to plant, his son gave him a cockerel, his wife Elizabeth presented a shirt and jacket, and, for Ruatara's wife Rahu, a red dress.

The physical evidence of two cultures entwining is especially vivid in artworks and architecture, even on the most traditional marae. Te Whiti's meeting house at Parihaka echoes a colonial settler's house. The prophet Rua Kēnana, who once foretold that all Pākehā would leave New Zealand, built an extraordinary circular meeting house and courthouse at Maungapōhatu in a remote corner of Te Urewera. This most sacred of Tūhoe places was decorated with a religiously symbolic painted yellow and blue playing card design. At Te Wairoa on Lake Tarawera, the meeting house replaced traditional shells with florins, shillings and sixpences. The painted interior of the wharenui at Rongopai Marae, built for Te Kooti outside Gisborne in 1887, features people, plants and even racehorses.

But the merging I love most is found in the tukutuku panels in Napier's Waiapu Cathedral. They form part of the Māori Chapel dedicated by Bishop Paul Reeves in 1977. Created as a project to help revive the then dying arts of weaving, dyeing and carving, they embrace a wonderful cultural mixture of symbols – chalices and crosses, stars and flounder, pūkeko footprints, albatross tears and monsters' teeth, woven into patterns known as mumu. The name comes from Māori watching a game of draughts played by Pākehā settlers as they sat outside a courthouse, waiting to buy land. And as they played, Māori thought they heard them say, 'Your move, your move … mumu, mumu.'

This cultural mixing and trimming can, though, also be ambiguous. Following the huge success of the movie based on it, Witi Ihimaera's novel *The Whale Rider* was reissued in an international edition with all the Māori words translated, and the Kiwi colloquialisms universalised and Americanised. So mates became buddies.

All of what has happened ever since the start of cultural contact, through all these comminglings, sets the stage for the hybridity now emerging – not a takeover or some new form of colonial control but an authentic meeting and mixing of cultures, fused into our art and music, and on television. Māori Television, which began broadcasting in March 2004, has the slogan 'Mā rātou, mā mātou, mā koutou, mā tatou' – For them, for us, for you, for everyone. The channel has made some outstanding programmes – its Anzac Day coverage is a case in point – and has won a considerable and faithful Pākehā audience. Like the rest of the Māori media sector, Māori Television would benefit from greater funding and what Minister for Māori Development Willie Jackson, himself a former broadcaster, refers to as 'a fairer slice of the pie', but there is no question about its unique role and point of difference. The opening graphics use images of the cosmos and the spirit world, mediated by elders and ancestors. Try that on TVNZ and they'd be seen as too spiritual, or a promo for a sci-fi series. But for all that distinctiveness, Māori Television is still creating an in-between space accessible to both cultures.

To navigate through hybridity, in-between people are needed, skilled in crossing the cultural divides and weathering the accusations that erupt, as they have constantly on Māori Television, for being too Māori and inaccessible to Pākehā, or not being Māori enough. (Interestingly, Pākehā are often accused of trying to be too Māori, but never of not being Pākehā enough.) Green MP Teanau Tuiono is one of those bridge builders, Ngāpuhi and Cook Islander, one of the two-thirds of New Zealand-born Pasifika with Māori whakapapa. Asked on radio if he was half and half, his reply was classic Kiwi. 'Nah bro. If anything I'm whole. I don't think anyone is half anything. If anything I'm double. If I was a beer I'd be Double Brown. If I was a flavour at the diary I'd be twice as nice but only half the price. I am two peas in the cultural pod.'

Hone Kaa lived out an altogether different way of being an in-between person. Though deeply embedded in the Māori world, fluent and eloquent in its language, he moved easily between the cultures. As I said when we unveiled his headstone, he was a broker – someone who could stay hopeful and committed and energetic even when the evidence said it was too hard to keep going, too damaged to fix. Issues like child abuse and violence, the odds against confiscated land being restored, even continuing the simplest conversations between alienated people, are all simply too much for most of us, but Hone had the courage and confidence, and the bloody-mindedness, to stand in the middle of conflict and impossible breakdowns, until a way ahead could be found – especially between Māori and Pākehā.

In-between people, who show us how to live with a foot in both and a word from each culture – in Native American parlance they're called edgewalkers – also provide us with a new language. The current bicultural debate sounds at times like a bad Western, riddled with goodies and baddies and racial stereotypes. Everything and everyone is described in oppositional, binary terms that don't match the reality of everyday life in Aotearoa. In-between people and the shared alliances they help to build will help both partners to find a better way of talking.

Paul Meredith is one of those people. He calls himself, however unfashionably, half-caste. Why, he asks, can't I be both Māori and Pākehā? With family and whakapapa links and historical memory deep in both cultures, he recalls with some embarrassment a photograph of a Meredith forebear holding a whip that belonged to the Prussian adventurer Gustavus von Tempsky, commander of the Forest Rangers during the New Zealand Wars. 'I used to wonder how many of my Māori relations faced this whip.' I can relate to his discomfort. My own great-great-grandmother ran a hostelry in Ardmore which the notorious colonel and his men used to frequent.

Meredith argues that the half-caste identity gives freedom to move between both cultures. 'I am not insisting that "Māori" must acknowledge and live their hybridity if that is not the particular identity they wish to adopt. However I do not expect Māori, Pākehā or whomever to deny those of us the privilege of adopting an identity that is both Māori and Pākehā. Nor do I welcome any proclamation as being disloyal or un-Māori/un-Pākehā. I can recall some people's bewilderment when I tell them to work out how I am Māori while at the same time how I am Pākehā.' For him, this confusion is 'a sad indictment on a society that seeks to categorise and stereotype each other around the principle of exclusion rather than inclusion'. Both cultures are needed; a mixing not a merging is required. We are, as Governor Hobson actually said, 'many peoples making up one nation'.

PART III

WAYS AHEAD

CHAPTER 19

That's what friends are for

He hono tangata, e kore e motu,
Kapa he taura waka, e motu.
A human bond cannot be parted
Unlike a canoe rope.

Friendship between Māori and Pākehā has had a sometimes hesitant history. It's difficult to find in te reo a word that fits precisely the English word for friend. These days the bicultural relationship perhaps tends to take the form of male mateship at work, sport and the pub, but stories of friendship have abounded since the beginning of Pākehā settlement. Diaries of the first missionaries, traders and settlers describe friendships with Māori that may have started with buying and selling, preaching or teaching, but developed into something enduring and heartfelt. Missionaries Henry Williams, Charles Reay, Octavius Hadfield and Thomas Grace, to name only a few, all achieved remarkable success in peacemaking through the credibility of their relationships with high-ranking chiefs.

George Selwyn's record is also remarkable, for all its flaws. Appointed by Queen Victoria to be the country's first Anglican bishop, he was torn between that loyalty and the growing claims of the Māori King movement, championed by his friend Wiremu Tamihana. At an 1862 hui at Tamihana's marae in Peria in Northland, Selwyn described himself as no longer the English gentleman who arrived in New Zealand 20 years before: 'I am not a Pākehā, neither am I a Māori; I am a half-caste. I have eaten your food, and I have slept in your houses; we have eaten together, talked together, travelled together, prayed together and partaken of the Lord's Supper together; and therefore I tell you I am a half-caste. My being a half-caste cannot be altered (or uprooted). It is in my body, in my flesh, in my sinews, in my bones, and in my marrow. We are all half-castes.'

Tamihana's response to the speech was to put two sticks in the ground, one for the Māori King, the other for the Crown, and to lay a third stick across them both, signifying the Christian faith they shared. It could equally have been a metaphor for their friendship, but it proved to be a hard challenge from a friend, asking for a loyalty that Selwyn struggled to give. Only a year later he felt compelled to act as chaplain to the British troops called to serve the same monarch who had appointed him. Selwyn was blamed for colluding in the massacre of women and children at the Battle of Rangiaowhia, falsely as it turned out. He was not even present at the time.

Archdeacon (later Bishop) Octavius Hadfield also had strong friendships with Māori and, like Selwyn, used equally passionate language to defend them in an 1861 letter to the editor of the *Times* of London regarding the Taranaki War. Governor Gore Browne, led by 'underhand and sinister influence' had 'blundered' into the conflict, which had as its 'real object … nothing less than the acquisition of 600 acres which the settlers were anxious to obtain'. Local Māori were 'fighting in support of law and order, in opposition to the illegal conduct of Governor Browne; and there can be no doubt that they are right in this view of the subject'. Only a year before, Hadfield had written an even stronger letter to the Duke of Newcastle, Secretary of State for the Colonies, warning Britain against starting a conflict that would become 'a war of races, which must be a war of extermination'. More British troops than Māori had been killed in earlier warfare in the 1840s. 'In a war of races the loss of life and the expenditure would be greater still. Is Great Britain prepared to purchase at such a price as this her own everlasting disgrace?'

As well as Pākehā defence of Māori rights, there were many Māori expressions of appreciation. In September 1863, as the New Zealand Wars raged, a group of Kaipara chiefs wrote a letter to 'our beloved friends, the Pākehās', which was printed in the local newspaper. Part of it read:

> We wish to live at peace with all men. We do not share the feelings of those foolish tribes who are sending away their Pākehās and with them all wisdom and useful knowledge. We do not wish to return to those customs of ignorance and darkness which we have left far behind, but rather to

reach to those heights of knowledge which our friends the Pākehās point out to us. If there be confusion in the North or South of this island, we have no sympathy with these things, but desire to live as in the days that are past, that is, in the light.

It's been a long time since anyone has talked about beloved Pākehā friends in Aotearoa. You would search in vain through the social media pages of the current debate to find anything like that sentiment. And you'd be lucky to find any Pākehā claim the right to belong here as boldly as Don Stafford of Rotorua did. A fluent speaker of te reo, respected for his history of the Arawa people, Stafford began a 2006 speech, 'I am here to talk about 1000 years of history in this place, and it is my history.' He could make that claim only because he had invested in a lifetime of friendship.

That part of the country is renowned for its cross-cultural friendships. In the early years of last century, Pākehā Florence Harsant was made Māori organiser for the Women's Christian Temperance Union, working in communities across the Bay of Plenty and Coromandel through difficult times, not least the 1913 smallpox epidemic, which killed 55 people. Harsant grew up in Taranaki and then Waitahanui near Taupo, where her father established a new Māori school. Known as Te Maari, after her second name of Marie, Harsant spoke te reo fluently and moved confidently within the Māori world of tikanga and tapu, kōrero and karakia, enjoying friendships and hospitality that defined her life until she died at 103.

In her life as a social worker and temperance campaigner, trekking through remote villages with a temperamental packhorse named Satan, Harsant ran into all sorts of hardships and rough customers, more often Pākehā than Māori. During a 1913 visit to Whakapara in the Far North, Harsant heard of two Māori women who were refused overnight stabling for their horses by the Pākehā proprietor 'because the Māoris have smallpox'. He grudgingly fed the animals outside. When the women returned to pick up their horses and the proprietor asked for payment, they were amused: their money might carry smallpox. 'Ah, that's different,' he replied. One woman threw the money on the ground and suggested that 'he could pick it up as the horses had had to pick up their feed'.

Harsant ends her memoir, published in 1979, with these words:

I have shared in the best of two worlds, pākehā and Māori.
And it would be less than honest not to say that at times
I have seen the least desirable features of both cultures,
though I must admit that in the case of the Māori people
many of those weaknesses have been pākehā-induced.

I am European. My skin is white; I cannot trace my
whakapapa back to the Great Fleet. But I do know that the
happiest years of my life were spent in the company of my
Māori friends.

Tell me, Rangi, Papa, elemental Gods – can a Māori
heart beat in a pākehā body?

CHAPTER 20

The two of us

The best way to discover what really happens when Pākehā and Māori meet and live together is to ask a bicultural couple. I persuaded three to entrust me with the story of their relationships, some of them spanning over 50 years. They are all public figures: Sir David and Lady Tureiti Moxon, Dr Waiora Port and her late husband, Garth, and Radio New Zealand's Paul Bushnell and his late partner, Dr Jonathan Mane-Wheoki. Their stories are all very different, and told in different voices, yet they share some revealing and highly personal insights into the unique, often delicate space that lies between the two cultures.

The Moxon whānau mostly live in Kirikiriroa/Hamilton, where Tureiti is the managing director of Te Kōhao Health, a Māori non-government agency. She also chairs the National Urban Māori Health Authority and is a member of the Waitangi Tribunal. Tureiti, who has a degree in law and a diploma in early childhood education, was previously a co-ordinator of the Kōhanga Reo movement, and worked as a lawyer. She was also a negotiator and trustee of the Ngāti Pāhauwera Development

Trust, who settled their Waitangi Tribunal claim with the Crown in 2012. David, now semi-retired, was the Anglican Bishop of Waikato and then Archbishop and Primate of the New Zealand dioceses. He later served as the Archbishop of Canterbury's representative to the Holy See and was Director of the Anglican Centre in Rome. He was knighted in 2014 and in 2020 made Priory Dean for Aotearoa New Zealand of the Order of St John Hato Hone Aotearoa.

Dr Waiora Port (Te Aupouri (Ngāti Pinaki) and Te Rarawa (Ngāti Maroki)) knows more about the bicultural life than most New Zealanders. After an earlier career as a teacher, she graduated with her first degree at 60, an MA Hons at 65 and a PhD at 74, researching Māori responses to DNA testing of those who had an inherited cancer. She has been a leader in medical research and public health work, including time as the kai arataki (cultural adviser) of Northern Regional Genetic Services, a member of the Bioethics Council, Toi Te Taiao, and co-chair of the Māori Advisory Board of Brain Research New Zealand. She was married to her Pākehā husband Garth for 60 years, until his death in 2014, and together they raised five daughters. Her achievements, she says, owe a lot to his interested support and encouragement.

For 35 years broadcaster Paul Bushnell shared his life with Jonathan Mane-Wheoki, of Ngāpuhi, Te Aupōuri, Ngāti Kurī and English descent, who was an international art scholar and teacher. Jonathan died in 2014 from pancreatic cancer, ending a distinguished career at Ilam Art School in Canterbury, Elam in

Auckland and Te Papa, as teacher, researcher, writer and mentor in the art worlds of Māori and Pākehā.

* * *

Whakapapa literally defines Māori: you are where you come from. For Pākehā, less so, perhaps. Tureiti Moxon, for example, introduces herself with a lineage that goes back to the arrival of the canoe Tākitimu around 1060. Her Hawkins whānau, on her father, Te Muera's, side, is from Ngāti Pāhauwera, a hapū of Ngāti Kahungunu in Te Matau-a-Māui, Hawke's Bay. Her marae is Te Waipapa-a-Iwi, her wharenui is Te Kahu o Te Rangi, her mountain is Tawhirirangi, and Maungaharuru, and Te Awa o Mōhaka is her river. She is also of Kāi Tahu descent in Te Wai Pounamu, the South Island, through her mother, Margaret Elizabeth Bashford.

David Moxon's whakapapa is shorter, but also proud. He was born in Papaioea, Palmerston North, and his father's family was English. But the Lancasters, Preeces and Lysnars on his mother's side come from Pākehā mission, education and farming lines who arrived here from England in 1831. Two of these forebears were present at the signing of Te Tiriti o Waitangi, and two of them, from 1846, were the first Pākehā to live in the Te Whāiti area of Te Urewera, where they founded an Anglican educational mission.

But however soundly connected Māori or Pākehā are in their whakapapa, claiming that identity is never straightforward. Waiora Port grew up in the Far North with a Māori mother and a Pākehā father, then, as an eight-year-old, moved to Auckland in the 1940s with her family, who were seeking a better life in the city, where there was plenty of work while so many men were away at war. She said: 'There weren't many Māori living in Auckland at that time but they seemed to be concentrated in the slum area of the inner city among Pākehā working-class people. The assimilationist policy imposed by the government from 1844 meant that Māori had to renounce their language and culture and be educated in the English traditions and language.'

When Waiora was enrolled at Napier Street School in Freemans Bay, with her younger sister, her experience was the opposite of Ahipara Native School, where there were few Pākehā pupils. 'Because our dad was Pākehā we had been known in Ahipara as "the Pākehā kids". At our new school we became "black Māori kids". We had not minded being called the Pākehā kids but I remember not liking being called the black Māori kids. Being Māori was not something that was valued, and I was always embarrassed if a teacher asked if there were any Māori in the class for whatever reason. Being Māori was always a feeling of being judged and a lack of pride in our culture became the default position.'

Waiora went on to Auckland Girls' Grammar School: 'I thrived, making the first eleven, but didn't achieve my potential scholastically.' Then came Auckland Teachers' College, where one Māori male student teacher remarked that he had never met a more 'Pākehā (fied) person'. Waiora 'did not feel comfortable with the Māori students, who all seemed so much better at things Māori than I was. I was happier with my Pākehā friends and so successful had my assimilation been, that I did not really think of them as Pākehā until I was at teachers' college, where there were so many more Māori than at my secondary school.'

Although Paul Bushnell knew that his partner Jonathan had a Māori father and an English mother, who had separated many years before, he didn't 'recall much talk early on about his Māori background and his childhood in Titirangi. With his sister Moea he grew up as one of the very few Māori children in the neighbourhood, and they made common cause with the Jews, the Dutch immigrants, and the children of the artist Colin McCahon due to their collective status as outsiders.'

As Paul suggests, 'because being Māori seemed not to be especially central to Jonathan, it never registered as a point of difference between us … He was my only close acquaintance who was Māori, for Christchurch then, as now, was very white.' In the couple's early years together, Jonathan was very supportive of a collective of Māori artists, but his interest in Māori contemporary art was only beginning to develop.

In Paul's words, Jonathan's relationship with his father was 'a slightly guarded one. Respectful on his father's side, slightly dutiful on Jonathan's side. Despite the obvious care they had for each other, there seemed to be quite a gulf between them.' But once, when he had taken his father out to dinner, a neighbouring diner commented that it was obvious that Jonathan's father 'loved him very much, and was very proud of him'. His death a few years later would prove pivotal.

With other family members, Jonathan travelled in the van with his father's coffin from Auckland to Piki Te Aroha Marae at Horeke in Hokianga, where the tangi was held. 'Going through that not only brought a sense of closure to what had been an important relationship, but it also provided reconnection with his whānau and iwi, and would prove central to his rediscovery of his Māori identity. It's as though it crystallised the previously somewhat inchoate sense of who he was.' Paul said Jonathan asked himself, 'What did it mean to stand here? What could an internationalist scholar and teacher bring to local stories, local histories? What illumination could he bring to the general audience about the renaissance in Māori art which seemed to be under way? The impact on Jonathan's teaching and research was profound. He retained a deep knowledge of nineteenth- and twentieth-century international art and architecture, but increasingly saw it as his role to document and explore the rise of contemporary Māori art, as well as that of the Pacific.'

Jonathan's childhood holidays were spent with his grandparents in the Far North. 'His father would carry all the family across the creek one by one after their long bus journey north [from West Auckland], and they would walk up the hill carrying their bags to their grandparents' whare with its floor made of beaten earth. His grandmother spoke only a few words of English. For that boy to end up studying in the UK, embracing the cosmopolitan high culture he found there, and feeling entirely a "citizen of the world" is remarkable.' And that journey happened in reverse: 'the older he got, the more Māori

Jonathan became.' When he died, a tangi at the University of Auckland marae was followed by a funeral service at Holy Trinity Cathedral and then a journey north to Piki Te Aroha Marae 'in a simple van, just as his father had been taken home decades before'.

Paul knows that he could not have made those decisions about that weekend of mourning, without 'a series of bicultural conversations in the months before. Some of them required the exercise of patience and cross-cultural tolerance which I could not have imagined myself making in the past. I had wise counsel from experts in te ao Māori to guide me through the complexities of both general protocols but also the likelihood of dealing with very specific problems ... The final details were worked through with Jonathan's wider whānau. There would be a way of honouring him which did no dishonour to both his Māori and Pākehā worlds.'

The tangi, Paul believes, is 'certainly something for Pākehā to learn from Māori. What I knew generally about the structure of Māori rituals of grief, connected easily to my own Irish Catholic background – especially in the transition from mourning to celebration and the importance of togetherness, food and time. But when you are at a tangi as the chief mourner, what you go through is both specific and powerful. All of this elaborate protocol, all the care and attention, the moments of formality and the times of relaxed togetherness, both recognises grief and provides a way of working through it.' The tangi, and the later unveiling of Jonathan's tombstone, changed Paul. 'And for a

Pākehā boy born in deepest Southland to be given the honour of lying beside Jonathan in that urupā, should that be my wish, is beyond extraordinary. If having a sense of place is about where you stand, how much more is that true of where you lie.'

Waiora Port's story is equally shaped by the experience of loved ones dying. When her Pākehā father died in 1974 and was buried in the family urupā, her husband Garth asked to be buried there himself one day. 'All the kaumatua who had seen Garth roaming the valley with our children nodded and smiled but one of my male cousins stood and very solemnly (tongue in cheek, I believe, or was it?) said, "*No*. By the time we die there will be no room because it will be too full of Pākehā." Forty years later Garth was buried in the urupā, in the basement suite as we called it, and I will be above him in the penthouse suite when my time comes.'

Waiora did not then feel that her life was 'lacking in the Māori dimension' because she and her family had kept their connections with her mother's whānau and turangawaewae. However, the death of her mother in 1966, when Waiora was 34, changed the course of her life.

'After great discussion within our family and her brothers and sister coming from the north to request her body for burial it was decided to return my mother's body to our turangawaewae and the urupā where all our close whānau were buried. At her tangi I realised for the first time that my identity as a brown Pākehā was challenged.' It happened when, as the eldest child, she was asked to thank everyone in the wharenui for all they had done for my mother's tangi. 'My shame at not being able to do this in Māori was so great that I vowed to learn my mother's birth language and one day be able to stand up and speak in Māori in that marae.'

But this was the mid-1960s and the Māori language renaissance had not begun. 'While it was so easy to articulate the words and the feelings about wanting to learn te reo, it was a long hard road of 18 years to acquire fluency in what should have been my birthright. These feelings have been echoed by people of other ethnicities and cultures who have come under the influence of European colonisation and assimilation. If you're black or brown in a white society, it's always a struggle to achieve the "bicultural competence" needed to succeed.'

* * *

For Tureiti and David Moxon, Te Tiriti o Waitangi is as central to their marriage and whānau life as it is to the nation. Their treaty-bound story is both complicated and demanding, living in what they call 'the engine room' of this bicultural country. As they say, both treaty partners are 'respectful and clear about their respective heritage by birth, and both seek to thrive from the unique strengths and gifts of each tikanga and culture. Blending one tikanga, one cultural way of life, totally into the other isn't an option. This means that the partners need to meet in the middle on common ground, without losing the uniqueness of the home of origin grounding with its whakapapa, lineage, and lore.' The same applies to what the Moxons call their 'post emancipation marriage'. As they point out, 'There is no easy road map ... There are, however, the principles of equity, rangatiratanga/ self-determination, options, partnership and protection that the treaty expresses, which provide the dynamics for our life together. These are not always immediately self-evident. They require constant communication and negotiation.'

Their approach is, they admit, 'more complex perhaps than some others, where one partner might identify mostly with the culture of the other rather than their own, or where both partners come from the same culture. Wanting the same thing for Aotearoa, for race relations, and for justice is the key.' It's a partnership 'full of energy, demand and progress, but not without some risk and tension', but it evolves 'because there are more positives than downsides.' And their marriage, whānau and wider community links wouldn't be viable without their shared faith. They quote an ancient whakatauaki, saying: 'Ko te amorangi ki mua, ko te hapai ki muri: Put what is sacred first and everything else will find its way.'

* * *

Jonathan Mane-Wheoki's story gives another glimpse into the subtlety of the codes that shape us all. As his Māori heritage became more defining, Paul remembers, 'he continued to use the research and writing skills developed in the Courtauld Institute in London where he had studied, but decided that it didn't make sense any more to be acting as if he were an academic working in a regional red-brick university in the UK, yearning for the "real life" in the metropolis of London.' Paul recognises now, too, how his partner's 'recharged sense of being Māori gave greater power and gravitas to his oratory'. He was already an accomplished communicator 'but it was in his off-the-cuff oratory that his Māori ancestry would most obviously play out'. Paul saw 'a deep vein of "present-ness"', which he has continued to experience in Māori life: 'The ability to weave together the disparate threads of the experience, to draw into that moment the past, and to acknowledge and celebrate those who are gathered in words fitting the occasion. The sense of recognising in a moment of transience deeper currents and significance.'

Although Jonathan's grasp of te reo continued to grow, he never felt expert in either the language or in tikanga. But Paul came to rely on his familiarity with both. 'When we were hanging around outside the McDougall Art Gallery for the opening of the *Te Māori* exhibition, I was impatient that nothing was happening. Why weren't formalities under way? Everyone was here so why no action? Jonathan told me to relax. "When you're at a Māori event, everything follows tikanga. Those in charge have to feel it's the right time to start." And so it proved.' Inside, Paul was startled to see the guides 'strewing greenery on or in front of the works on display, and touching them as they talked to visitors about their connection with them'. But Jonathan reassured him that this, too, was fine. As Paul puts it, 'The traditional "don't touch" values of the Eurocentric art museum are not the only values which matter.' Yes, these artefacts were works of high art, but they were grounded 'in this place, in this culture, and in a story which winds back far beyond the arrival of Pākehā'.

As Jonathan began to turn his skill as a researcher and writer to Māori subjects, the results 'would undercut colonial history and attitudes. He infuriated some older Pākehā artists by his coverage of the "young guns" – the new generation of Māori artists. He shocked one audience by declaring that the master weaver Dame Rangimārie Hetet was the country's greatest living artist.' He also put his primary research abilities 'to the task of revealing uncomfortable truths about the annexation of Māori culture'. His Waitangi Tribunal report into the Ngāti Awa meeting house, Mataatua, 'established, for the first time, "a full and unbroken chronology" for this wharenui, explaining how it ended up in the Otago Museum, and providing unassailable evidence of bad faith and broken promises by representatives of the Crown over the century since it was uplifted from Whakatāne'.

Jonathan never pushed himself forward in terms of academic promotion, which Paul now sees as 'not only an individual preference, but something deeply Māori. He embodied the whakatauki that the kumara does not brag about its own sweetness: Kāore te kumara e kōrero ana mo tōna ake reka.' Jonathan also 'refused to play the "snakes and ladders" game of academic preferment. If a position was offered, he might take it, but he would never suggest it himself.'

* * *

For Waiora Port, identity comes from a rich cultural entanglement that she's sometimes had to fight to defend. 'I have often wondered why God made black people and others with shading going lighter and lighter. Everything living has DNA. More and more different cultures are coming to Aotearoa and inevitably people will choose partners cross-culturally. Marriage does mean we get to know more about each other's culture and we can choose the best of each if we wish. I love so many things Māori that Garth and I were delighted to share; but I have also read, listened and been enraptured with English literature and poetry in particular, and glorious church music. He taonga.'

She wondered why her mother-in-law uttered the words, 'The bloods won't mix.' 'As training college students we were asked to volunteer a Friday morning in Symonds Street in Auckland trying to talk people into being blood donors. Luckily my friend had a brother working in an office close by and we signed some young men from there. I also asked Garth to sign up. (We were both A Rh Positive.) I could not resist saying, "Please also inform your mother it is not blue."'

Waiora is delighted to observe more Māori–Pākehā marriages happening 'without the upsets we faced nearly 70 years ago. My sister's romance broke off because her boyfriend, although Māori–Dalmatian, could not come to our wedding because he was Catholic … My dad would not allow him to miss the service and come to the reception as he was allowed to do. I remember vowing that if any of our children came home with friends of different religious beliefs or nationalities who might be prospective partners I would be welcoming and take time to get to know them.' Even when her daughters have remarried, Wairoa remains friends with their former husbands and is 'great friends' with her sons-in-law, and her 11 mokopuna (grandchildren) and four mokopuna tuarua (great-grandchildren). 'For me the bloods have mixed well. That's proved by my daughters and our two generations of mokopuna visiting me online every morning, all keeping in touch. Ko te mea nui – he tangata, he tangata, he tangata he tangata. It's people who matter.'

* * *

The bicultural relationships that produce children bring promise and hope for a very different Aotearoa. The Moxon marriage has produced 'four tamariki, children, and three mokopuna, grandchildren, who all speak te reo Māori. They all identify as Ngāti Kahungunu and Kāi Tahu. They were raised to identify as Māori, with a bicultural Pākehā heritage.' Tureiti and David quote the words of Apirana Ngata:

> *E tipu, e rea, mō ngā rā o tō ao; ko to ringaringa ki ngā rākau*
> *a te Pākehā hei oranga mō tō tinana; ko tō ngākau ki ngā*
> *taonga o ō tīpuna hei tikitiki mō tō māhunga.*
> *Ko tō wairua ki tō Atua, nāna nei ngā mea katoa.*
>
> *Grow tender shoots for the days of your world; turn your hand*
> *to the tools of the Pākehā for the well-being of your body;*

*turn your heart to the treasures of your ancestors as a crown for
your head.*
Give your soul unto God the author of all things.

The Moxon children 'identify strongly with Māori heritage
because this is who they are. They draw on the ancient cultural
uniqueness of these islands, and the rich bicultural space this
offers them and others today. They are a bridge between the
cultures and from this way of life into the wider world. This
also means that their friends and colleagues can find the passage
easier and more fruitful between the races.'

* * *

The last voice in this chapter, the voice of a friend, is anonymous
because his bicultural family decided it was not the right time to
be telling their stories. There were fears that their mana might
suffer from publishing the details of entwining Māori and
Pākehā whakapapa. These fears took me by surprise, though
they shouldn't have. I've already told of the stories in my own
family, an uncle fathering a Māori daughter, that were never
spoken about. Bicultural relationships, however mainstream
they might have become, still hold this anxiety about how they
will be received and interpreted in both cultures.

My friend's bicultural marriage of three decades ended in
divorce but another decade later, he continues to be involved in
the lives of his children and former partner and her whānau.
When he married he was told he was also marrying a tribe and

that remains true. He is still welcomed on the home marae and has never been made to feel a stranger. His Pākehā ancestral faith continues to be woven for him into Māori spirituality. His own family dates back to the earliest days of colonial settlement. His great-great-grandfather was a well-known cavalry officer who fought in several campaigns in the land wars across the North Island.

My friend grew up on a farm near a provincial town and interacted easily with Māori families in school and church and sports. His parents were happily part of this interaction, though something happened to change that, a dramatic illustration of the way in which both Māori and Pākehā are shaped by subtle patterns of behaviour buried in their respective cultures, often barely within their awareness. He had begun a high school romance with a fellow student from a local Māori family. 'We had been out to the pictures a couple of times, talked at school, shared lunches and supported our mutual sports teams. She lived in town. I was 10 miles away out in the country.' Then one day his girlfriend turned up unannounced at the family farm: her parents were heading out for the day and would pick her up upon their return. 'We were having lunch, and simultaneously we all saw her coming across the lawn. My parents said casually, "I wonder who this is?" I sat there blushing and said it was a friend from school.' Looking back, my friend asks, 'Would it have mattered if she were Pākehā? Probably not, but it didn't help that she was "Maari", as the name was mispronounced. It was more the fact that her parents had dropped her at the gate without coming in or making some pre-arrangements that horrified my parents. Her family knew me and I knew them. Fine by me, but not so for my parents ... What sort of family would drop their teenage daughter off at a stranger's home in the country? It reinforced all my parents' prejudices ... Did this incident show more about my family than the wider culture? Whichever it was, it was a pivot point of difference for me.'

The difference continued to define my friend's life. Years later, when serving with the New Zealand Defence Force, he was welcomed, along with other officers, to the historic St Mary's Church in New Plymouth, which housed many memories of the Taranaki wars. Archdeacon Tiki Raumati led the welcoming pōwhiri. 'Though welcome is a slight stretch of the imagination. Tiki's whaikōrero at the threshold of St Mary's left one reaching for courage to pick up the wero and advance. In short, he reminded us that our uniforms were symbols of the colonisation that led to the destruction of his whānau, hapū, iwi, all within sight of their maunga, Taranaki. We were left in no doubt of our pedigree, past carnage, and his passion for wrongs to be addressed.'

Eventually the officers were seated in the church. 'I can't say the doors were bolted, but bolting was not an option.' Above them the regimental colours and coats of arms were displayed on the walls, as were brass plaques remembering officers who had led and served the regiment; the soldiers responsible for Parihaka and the atrocities, te pāhua, on 5 November 1881. My friend, pointing to a plaque to the regiment's commanding officer, whispered to a colleague sitting with him, 'Not a good time to point out he's my great-great-grandfather?' The colleague agreed, warning that 'I might be thrown out with all my family memorabilia'.

On reflection, my friend appreciates the ferocity of that welcome and the courage taken by mana whenua even to consider welcoming those uniforms back. He wonders now, two decades later, whether the organisers understood what the uniforms meant in that divisive context. In te ao Māori style, what followed was fierce whaikōrero, passionate truth-speaking, karakia with conciliatory prayers, Gospel (Kauhau), then food, hospitality, and a blessing to send the chaplains on their way.

For my friend's bicultural whānau, Taranaki is a discombobulated place, but St Mary's has changed. The church, now Taranaki Cathedral, has been restored and strengthened, and the regimental colours removed for the time being and preserved by the army. A new attached building, Te Whare Hononga – the House that Binds – developed with Ngāti Te Whiti, will be devoted to the work of peace and reconciliation and tell the story of local iwi, Ngāti Te Whiti, Atiawa and Taranaki, and their links with the church and with the land on which it stands. And Archdeacon Tiki, who later became the cathedral's first kaumātua, and died in 2018, lies in the graveyard outside the door, one of only three people to have been buried there in the last 50 years.

* * *

My friend's story is difficult for him to tell, but it's also a hopeful story. He looks forward to a very different Aotearoa. 'Having adult children and grandchildren who are bicultural in whakapapa and nature helps me to be culturally aware and competent. Unlike my parents' generation, we can talk about Aotearoa's cultural issues and how they will change society' and those conversations, though not always easy, will not be 'tokenistic and layered with paternalism'. There are issues regarding unmet Māori aspirations that 'make it painful to be a Pākehā who is bicultural', but 'future generations of my whānau will not have to feel uncomfortable as tangata whenua, like those who have gone before them. Yes, I know we have a way to go, and I will grow with them.'

CHAPTER 21

Shared stories that won't let us go

Being bicultural isn't for sissies – it's an obstacle course – but despite all the forces that work against Māori and Pākehā alliances, they still flourish. And when they do, everyone watching is encouraged and enriched. Telling the stories of these alliances can be a game changer, especially when fears abound, driven by social media gossip and mutual ignorance. Personal experiences dissolve the theories and legalities, the grievances and inequalities, the lack of understanding that makes both cultures stumble and that work to keep them apart. Sometimes the story is told very formally and institutionally as a legal covenant, a governing constitution, a business mission statement. But, rather more subtly and more intriguingly, the story is also embedded in statues and signposts, places and place names, symbols and rituals, events and festivals, art and music.

It's hard to imagine the popular music scene in Aotearoa today without Māori lyrics, songs and voices. But it wasn't always so. Although there had been local and overseas concert parties and performers before then, Māori music was often most often heard on marae. It was the two world wars that had a lot to do with its wider emergence. In 1914, for an official government publication called *Songs, Haka and Ruri for the Use of the Māori Contingent*, Āpirana Ngata and Hone Heke Ngapua translated popular patriotic songs and ballads into Māori. Among them – full of pride in empire that feels far away today, but was real and proudly sung about back then – were 'Nga Hoia a te Kuini/ Soldiers of the Queen' and 'Maranga ki Runga/Tramp, Tramp, Tramp, the Boys are Marching'. The return of the Māori Pioneer Battalion in 1919 drew huge welcoming crowds in Auckland on a scale not seen since the royal visit of 1901. And where the men marched they sang songs that had joined the musical repertoire of the whole nation.

In the next world war the Māori Battalion continued that tradition and their song was familiar to every child, whether Māori or Pākehā, in the 1950s. We all knew they marched to glory and took the honour of the country with them. And when they left, they were farewelled with another song everyone knew, 'Now is the Hour/Po Atarau', an Australian tune that had been given Māori words by Maewa Kaihau back in 1926. 'Blue Smoke' was an even bigger bicultural hit. It was written by dance band pianist Ruru Karaitiana on the troopship *Aquitania* off the coast of Africa in 1940, after a passing sergeant pointed out the smoke drifting from the ship's funnels back towards New Zealand. Although it was performed regularly throughout the war, the song found its real fame in 1949 when Karaitiana's quintet recorded a version, sung by Pixie Williams. As Chris Bourke says, it was 'the first complete New Zealand pop song ... written, recorded and manufactured locally, then commercially released on a new label dedicated to New Zealand artists'. It became an international hit overnight – local sales could have been as high as 50,000 – and Dean Martin added it to his repertoire.

Thirty-five years later, in 1984, the Pātea Māori Club launched 'Poi E', which proved even more iconic for Māori and Pākehā alike. Few other songs in our history have such an effect on popular culture. The blend of traditional Māori voices and rhythms, mixed with show band, funk, hip hop and gospel influences, sent the song to the top of the charts and made it the best-selling recording of the year. Written by Ngoi Pēwhairangi, and scored and produced by Maui Dalvanius Prime, the song was labelled New Zealand's unofficial national anthem.

* * *

Other arts forms are equally powerful as a medium for expressing bicultural connection. Is it because they can avoid the entanglements and constraints of verbal language and speak to the heart of the matter through imagination, patterns, shapes and colours?

Back in the 1990s, a proposed new visitors' centre alongside the Neo-Gothic cathedral in the centre of what was then called the 'most English of cities', incurred the full fury of the Christchurch architectural establishment. By selecting a contemporary design – from Hamilton, just to make it worse – I and others offended the cultural dignity of Canterbury which, back then, was wholly defined by a Victorian heritage. Over years of public battle, played out on the editorial and letters page of the Christchurch *Press*, no one ever mentioned Ngāi Tahu, who had been around for a little longer.

Even as the first buildings in that Pākehā colonial story were emerging, artist Charles Haubroe was painting, in watercolour, the distinctly designed whare of Aperahama Te Aika, a chief of the hapū Ngāi Tūāhuriri, at Kaiapoi in North Canterbury. The same design, featuring high, crossed bargeboards, was unique to Ngāi Tahu and found on marae all around the South Island. Today that architectural tradition is honoured in the centre of the city, without any of the public outcry about art for which Christchurch has sometimes been known: the 1948 fiasco over the Frances Hodgkins painting *Pleasure Garden*, for example, or the public rejection of a 1972 plan to erect a Henry Moore sculpture on the Port Hills. No outcry now, but plenty of grumbling.

'The worst thing about public art is the public part,' says artist Wayne Youle, Ngāpuhi, Ngāti Whakaeke and Ngāti Pākehā, who is responsible for some stunning video artworks and signage around Christchurch. 'Look Mum, no hands', 'Wish you were here', 'Piece of mind', and 'Drum Roll Please' are just some of the messages he's sharing. The last one is especially powerful, anticipating, as it does, something unexpected ahead. Just the thing for an earthquake-broken city. Youle's work is ground-breaking preparation for a new era of art for Canterbury, where Ngāi Tahu's voice is becoming as visible aesthetically as it already has become commercially. Lonnie Hutchinson, an artist with Ngāi Tahu, Samoan and Pākehā heritage, is another indigenous presence in the post-earthquake cityscape. Her 36-metre-long cloak of kākāpō feathers fashioned from anodised aluminium transforms the new justice and emergency precinct.

Just as dramatic is the sculpture that forms the entranceway or ngutu to the new Christchurch Convention Centre, Te Pae. Entitled *Te Aika*, which translates as the home people, a Ngāi Tahu extension of keeping the home fires burning, it was produced by SCAPE Public Art and Matapopore, which brings together Ngāi Tūāhuriri and Ngāi Tahu experts to work alongside local and central government in ensuring a mana whenua voice and presence in the rebuilding of the city. *Te Aika* is the work of Ngāi Tahu artists Rachael Rakena and Simon Kaan, who drew their inspiration from the design in the Haubroe watercolour with the crossed barge boards, then added the idea of a kahukahu (feathered cloak) offering a protective embrace, mana and warmth. There's also the suggestion of the outstretched wings of the kōtuku (white heron). The ngutu, eight metres high and 10 metres wide, built out of steel panels, aluminium clad, and coated with a white textured feather-like surface, is a bold new bicultural statement in the heart of what was once the most monocultural of cities.

Sometimes it's an object as simple as a piece of clothing that carries the bicultural story most eloquently. Take the kaitaka or cloak of Rewi Manga Maniapoto, the famous paramount chief, statesman and military leader who in 1864 led Ngāti Maniapoto forces, 300 of them, against the 1400 British troops in the Battle of Ōrakau, an event popularised in the famous early New Zealand movie *Rewi's Last Stand*. Fourteen years later, Rewi made peace with the Crown and worked to rebuild the trust that had been broken by the war. As part of that reconciling, he gifted his precious cloak, treasured as a chiefly taonga, to a Pākehā neighbour, Thomas Grice. The story then takes a strange turn. Somehow the kaitaka ended up in England, with family members returning there, and was lost from the memory of everyone but Ngāti Maniapoto. A hundred and forty years later, the priceless kaitaka was rediscovered, tucked away in a linen closet in a Grice family house in Sussex. Through the network of the Anglican Church here and in England, its return was negotiated and Ngāti Maniapoto received it back into their care, with great rejoicing, at Ōrakau in 2021.

Stories like this don't often make the headlines, but they form part of a slow but constant movement to right the wrongs and restore the mana of precious things that were wrongly, mistakenly or thoughtlessly taken and need to be returned, for the sake of the giver and the receiver alike. Mokomokai (preserved tattooed heads), artworks, carving and weaving sold or taken to overseas collectors, books, photos, jewellery … The list of Māori and Pākehā treasures awaiting attention and redress is long.

* * *

I wonder what happened to the symbols that the prophet Tahupōtiki Wiremu Rātana presented to Prime Minister Michael Joseph Savage in Parliament buildings in 1936? It was a historic meeting of two cultures, made possible only by the mutual trust and respect between the men, despite the political tensions between them. The whole encounter was conducted through the language of symbols more than words, and delivered by Rātana.

He presented Savage with three objects. First, there were three huia feathers stuck into a kūmara. The feathers spoke of Māori native heritage. This bird was now extinct, destroyed by pests introduced by Pākehā. The kūmara was a reminder that Māori had no land left to plant such food. The second gift was a greenstone tiki representing the power and authority now lost to Māori through European laws. And finally, there was a broken gold watch and chain that had belonged to his grandfather, who, loyal to the government though he was, had no money to replace the broken glass. 'And nor have I,' said Rātana.

Savage's reply didn't avoid the judgement made by the symbols and he promised action. 'I take it upon myself to remedy those wrongs and injustices in a manner as near as possible to that required by the spirit of the Treaty of Waitangi ... Listen well, Ratana, only by removing the chains that bind and restrain the Māori people will I be able to say I have accomplished something in this land.' A month later the famous alliance began that was to shape New Zealand politics for a century, between the Labour Party and the Rātana Church.

* * *

Sometimes it's a symbol that cradles the trust between the cultures. Sometimes it's a place that speaks of that trust, both in its making and its breaking. Te Ngutu o te Manu (The Beak of the Bird) outside Whanganui is such a place for me. It's the site of the famous Ngāti Ruanui chief Riwha Tītokowaru's pā and the place where Manurau, the bird that flits everywhere – otherwise known as Gustavus von Tempsky – was killed along with 19 of his soldiers in September 1868. A Prussian military officer, adventurer, gold miner and journalist, Tempsky headed the Forest Rangers, who hacked a well-publicised path through the New Zealand Wars. But Māori respected this ruthless and much romanticised figure: Tītokowaru burned his body, and those of other soldiers, on a funeral pyre at his marae. Tempsky embodies a part of our history that is wrapped in Pākehā myth-making as much as Māori legend, which only makes it harder to grasp the full extent of the trauma and lasting damage of the New Zealand Wars.

That haunting is palpable at Te Ngutu o te Manu. A heart-shaped circle of trees encloses a mown paddock with a simple white cross and memorial stone to mark the graves. There is no trace of the bluster and heroics that marked Tempsky's colourful career. This is a simple, subdued and quiet place. Unlike other war memorials in Taranaki, there are no grand claims of victory and glory or accusations of savagery. This is a place of restraint for remembering the horror of what happened. The only splash of colour in the clearing comes from the bright plastic slides on the children's playground to one side of the enclosure where, I hope, Māori and Pākehā children play together.

There is another place that is almost as haunting, and speaks of broken trust in this bicultural partnership. You get to it by following a winding track – not a legal road, its possible upgrade became the subject of great controversy in 2000 – that takes you to the sacred mountain of Maungapōhatu in Te Urewera above Lake Waikaremoana. This was where Rua Kēnana set up his model township, complete with its own banking system, parliament building and pastoral farming economy. From this New Jerusalem, Rua built a new legacy of hope for his dispirited people and challenged the government of the day on everything from dog taxes to conscription for military service. They responded with a police raid on the settlement in 1916, which killed Rua's son Toko and his close friend. Rua and several others were arrested; the prophet himself was imprisoned. The raid marked the last armed conflict in a war with Māori that had begun 50 years before.

The marae at Maungapōhatu is another of those silent, brooding places that holds so much of the pain from a broken relationship that is only now slowly beginning to be restored. During the overnight visit I made there, as part of one of the first Pākehā groups to be invited, we heard terrible stories from the elders about the trauma of that 1916: they spoke as if it had taken place yesterday and the memories still drew tears.

In his book *Nothing Ever Dies*, about the Vietnam (he would say American) War, seen through Vietnamese eyes, Viet Thanh Nguyen uses the term 'just remembering'. He argues that the ethics of remembering are about the dialectic of memory and amnesia. We're good at remembering our humanity and forgetting our inhumanity. Pākehā are still in the early stages of working that out, as the Maungapōhatu story demonstrates.

One obvious reason is that Pākehā are humiliated and shamed by their failures, both in peace and war. New Zealand's worst ever military defeat was at Gallipoli; later came Passchendaele. New Zealanders dealt with Gallipoli by turning it into a national coming of age myth. Passchendaele is another story. It took 80 years before this terrible event was written about extensively in Glyn Harper's 2000 book, *Massacre at Passchendaele*. There are very few public memorials in New Zealand to record this country's worst military disaster and probably its worst disaster of any kind. In just a few hours, on 12 October 1917, more men, 843, died than on any other day in our bicultural history and many of the 1860 wounded did not recover.

To forget it is one strategy for dealing with a difficult past. To rearrange the story is another, or remembering selectively, as Pākehā still do with the New Zealand Wars and the land confiscations that followed. Constant challenging, rewriting and retelling are needed, and the work on the new history curriculum is trying to do that.

Efforts to increase the teaching in schools of our own history have been around since the 1940s. There was always a British version of that history on offer. I remember the map of the world on the primary school wall in Nūhaka, with the empire painted red, looking down on us. Sitting at our desks, we chanted aloud the whole country's coastal features, all Dutch and English names, from Cape Maria van Diemen down to Bluff. To rewrite the history curriculum, with its colonial framing, proved to be a much bigger job, taking over half another century, delayed by the advent of Tomorrow's Schools, which devolved us away from central planning. Curriculum reform was finally prompted by local communities rather than head office expertise.

A group of Ōtorohanga College students helped to lead the way. Back in 2014, after a confronting school visit to the battle sites of Ōrakau and Rangiowhia, they started a petition to have the New Zealand Wars taught in schools and remembered with a national day. The petition, which gathered 13,000 signatures, was presented to Parliament in 2016. A response from the Ministry of Education was underwhelming: it considered curriculum changes were unnecessary and 'likely to result in significant, negative and systemic consequences'. Journalist Philip Matthews charted what followed as the campaign continued until 2019, when Prime Minister Jacinda Ardern recognised a gathering grassroots movement for change. That prompted the project that produced a new curriculum released for public consultation in February 2021 and due to be implemented in 2023. All this was driven by both Māori students, teachers and academics and Pākehā, such as the New Zealand History Teachers' Association and its chair Graeme Ball, who served on the project's working group.

After wide consultation with schools, the proposal was narrowed down from seven to a more manageable three themes. The public response, when it came, was vociferous and vast:

4523 submissions in reply to a modest 11-page draft. The Royal Society Te Apārangi sent 24 pages of objections. One of the calmer voices belonged to historian Jock Phillips: 'It would be a tragedy if the planned curriculum simply evoked hostility and racist resentment because non-Māori New Zealanders found no place for their own traditions and experience. We must all know something about the impact of colonialism on Māori, but we should even more learn to love the multi-faceted history of this country and want to keep discovering it for ourselves.'

Having once made Māori invisible in our history or reduced them to a romanticised accessory, some Pākehā now say that too much is being made of their story, while glossing over unpleasant parts. Take, for example, the intertribal Musket Wars of the 1810s to the 1830s. Former leader of the National Party Don Brash demanded to know why they didn't feature, given, he claimed, that more died in them than any other conflict, though his quoted figures ranged widely. Graeme Ball, Chair of the NZ History Teachers' Association, answered that charge by saying those wars will be included, while reminding people that story is about trade as well as war, shaped by the arrival of muskets traded for food for settlers, especially the easily tradeable and portable potato.

The complaints also attacked what was left out, everything from women's history to popular culture. Starting with only three themes was bound to please no one. It was as though we decided to plant a new vegetable garden because the old one was no longer producing what we all needed to nourish us. There was room for only so many plants in the new plot, but the project stalled because 10 times more plants were demanded.

Nothing matched the fury of those who smelt a conspiracy to create white guilt and demonise Pākehā. The reactions revealed just how little most Pākehā New Zealanders knew about this country's colonial history, hardly surprising for a subject that schools had ignored for so long. As Pākehā struggled with their feelings about this impending sea change in the curriculum, few stopped to wonder how Māori might be feeling about all this. Their culture, in times of war and peace, had been largely ignored in the syllabus for a century and more. Māori students had had to absorb a story that made them largely invisible, bit players at best.

Ball defended the proposal, evolving as it is, saying it was not politically driven, but simply an attempt 'to look at our history in a more balanced way and that necessarily means giving more prominence to a marginalised voice'. But to do that is going to require not just a curriculum rewrite but also a rethink of how to teach the subject, so Māori and Pākehā students alike can be involved in the learning. Michael Harcourt's 2020 thesis, looking at the teaching and learning in secondary schools of New Zealand's difficult history of colonisation, offers an extensive survey of the hurdles that students and teachers alike have to jump in coming to terms with this country's colonial past. He found that teachers, though mostly open and sympathetic to the challenge and willing to deal critically with subject, underestimated the complexity involved. Students were divided on both the risks and the desire to learn. Young Pākehā often found it emotionally hard to come to terms with their history.

The whole undertaking will demand new ways of learning and teaching and closer consultation with those who hold both sides of the colonial story. Schools introducing the new curriculum will become bellwethers for the rest of the country in coming to terms with its history.

* * *

This growing pressure to rethink the way we learn and tell each other about our shared stories stretches across the whole canvas of our national life, from our streets, named as they are, to signs and statues. And when anyone tries to change them, erase or at least ease the evidence of colonial mistakes, there's a rash of letters to the editor.

As historian Paul Moon reminds us, things aren't as bad as in the United States – 'We don't have that extremist fervour here. We don't have people gathering around a statue of Sir George Grey and saying "The wars in the 1860s were wonderful"' – but we do have controversy. At the war memorial in Matakana near where I live, the statue of King George V has been decapitated five times; finally, a fibreglass version was added. In Hamilton, in 2020, the council removed the statue of the man who gave his name to the city from the central Civic Square after requests from the local iwi and threats from kaumātua Taitimu Maipi, who called the soldier a 'murderous arsehole'. Captain John Hamilton was one of the naval officers attending Archdeacon

Brown's dinner party on the eve of the Battle of Gate Pa in 1864. They all died the next day. Addressing the city councillors, Maipi asked, 'Would you have a street named after someone who came and murdered your family?' He is also targeting some Hamilton street names for change, including Von Tempsky, Bryce and Grey. The city itself is beginning to use its original name, Kirikiriroa.

Auckland has an even more contentious statue, though there are as yet no plans to remove it, despite calls to do so. Thirteen metres high, Colonel Marmaduke Nixon overlooks the traffic in Ōtāhuhu on the corner of Mangere and Great South roads. It was down the latter that Nixon led his troops to Waikato and the attack on Rangiaowhia. He later died from wounds received in that battle, which involved the burning of a whare where defenders had gathered. There were women and children among the dozen or so Māori who were killed. The debate over nixing the Nixon memorial still sways between those who want it removed, those who want it relocated and those who favour recontextualising it by adding additional plaques that acknowledge the two sides of the war story, both fighting for a country and a monarch. The shared story is as hard as ever to tell – so hard that the Māori Party has called for a government inquiry into reviewing and removing of statues. Until that happens, the slow shift to names that honour both indigenous and later histories will help to ease the tension.

* * *

Annie Proulx's novel *That Old Ace in the Hole* tells the story of Bob Dollar's adventures down in the Texas panhandle, a bleak and godforsaken landscape. For a while he stays in Woolybucket, a washed out, one-horse town on Route 444 – but not as far as the locals are concerned. The highway sign says, 'This is the best place in the world'. Wherever Bob drives, he finds, as well as non-verbal signs – dead cows by the roadside, legs stiff as two-by-fours, a plywood Jesus, an irrigation rig still decked in Christmas lights – other notices that are easier to read: 'The Town Where No One Wears a Frown', 'The Richest Land and the Finest People', '10,000 Friendly People and One or Two Old Grumps'.

Our signs are almost as colourful. Wairoa in Northern Hawke's Bay once labelled itself 'The way New Zealand used to be', Dunedin said 'It's all right here' and the Bealey Pub on the way to Arthur's Pass boasted a roadside warning 'Moa Crossing'. They go downhill from there – from Dannevirke's 'Take a Liking to a Viking' down to the Hutt Valley's 'Right up my Hutt Valley' and down again to Bulls' 'Herd of Bulls – a town like no udder'. Then we've got towns that promote themselves with giant fibreglass objects – a gumboot, a leaping salmon, an L & P bottle – and entering and exiting messages of 'Haere Mai' and 'Haere Ra'. There was a brief trial of stop/go signs in te reo in the Bay of Plenty, but Māori heritage features lightly in public signage and in some places not at all. The signs and names we wear on our sleeves as a country tell us, and the wider world, who we think we are. So do the media campaigns of advertisers trying to sell us something. Nescafé ads back in the 1960s were among the first to show Māori and Pasifika faces; now we see them on television every night.

Signs are easy to erect and change. Festivals and public events that celebrate our bicultural journey take more time to create and sustain. We could do with a few more that let both cultures feel at home with each other but they're hard to find yet.

CHAPTER 22

Biculturalism built in

For Pākehā, biculturalism is about being sympathetic; for Māori, it's about power sharing. And when it comes to the structure of our institutions, the tyres in this debate start to grip, because that's all about making partnership permanent, long term, sharing not just sympathies and personal bonds, but profit sharing and decision making. That kind of power is enshrined in law but rarely in the constitutions and founding documents of schools and universities, companies and councils, museums and charitable trusts. So the few examples become beacons of a very different and enduring future for Aotearoa.

Any discussion about institutional biculturalism needs to start at the top. Despite being a country of many cultures with the Treaty of Waitangi as its founding document, our constitution, unwritten though it is, is still decidedly British, with Queen Elizabeth as head of state, and a Parliament making laws that can't be tested by the courts or any independent body. The treaty and its principles of partnership, though legally recognised, is not a constitutional document. In Sir Geoffrey Palmer's words, the treaty is 'half in and half out of the legal system'. So the debate is whether it should be right in, like something akin to a superior law; or subordinate to a written constitution, alongside the Bill of Rights and other human rights declarations about housing, education and healthcare. Should there be some sort of upper house to ensure the treaty's principles are honoured?

That was the agenda for the conference on Building the Constitution held in Parliament buildings in 2000. It was a controversial gathering, fuelled by media coverage that largely ignored the actual agenda. A *Woman's Weekly* billboard at the time described it as a 'secret plot to abolish the Queen'. Sir Paul Reeves, who chaired the conference, wrote afterwards in the official report: 'The organisers found themselves charged with elitism, barely concealed agendas for change, encouragement for Māori separatism, let alone republicanism. The charges which came from all sorts of directions convinced me that our focus was about right.' Despite that good beginning, the debate hasn't progressed far. The foreshore and seabed furore that followed four years later highlighted the risk of not having clarity about the basics of ownership and governance. The succession of attempted and successful coups d'état in neighbouring Fiji and the resulting rewrite of their constitution in 2013 giving equal, though still disputed, status to all Fijians, was another warning of how deep the waters of constitutional reform might be.

Former Labour leader Mike Moore, once opposed to any written constitution, much later changed his mind. 'The Treaty is to the constitution what the Ten Commandments are to the

New [actually the Old] Testament. Without it what is there?' Moore saw the reform as necessary, but not immediately. 'We have the space,' he told the *Sunday Star Times* in 1998. 'There's no great urgency, because we're not ripping each other's throats out. It's the old question of when do you fix the roof? When the sun is shining or when it's pouring with rain? Most societies fix the roof too late.'

Is the currently overheated state of the bicultural debate a sign of more showers or a thunderstorm? And should the campaign to make New Zealand a republic gather strength, the constitutional debate will quickly revive. The Anglican Church attempted to do just that, following its success in adopting a bicultural constitution in 1992, the first New Zealand institution to do so. Honouring the treaty by giving tikanga Māori and Pākehā equal status and voice, it also made provision for a third tikanga, Pasifika, given the long connection with Pacific mission. All the church's big decisions are made in a General Synod/Te Hinota Whanui that acts as a kind of parliamentary upper house.

The church launched a nationwide discussion offering three possible models but the government of the day wasn't interested in adopting the model for the country as a whole. When Archbishop Whakahuihui Vercoe and Professor Whatarangi Winiata attempted to pursue the proposal further at a meeting with Prime Minister Jenny Shipley at Parliament to present the demands of the Hikoi of Hope in 1994, the discussion was shut down firmly. Shipley wasn't alone in her views. Few Pākehā politicians venture into that debate, even today.

Other institutions that have attempted to adopt bicultural constitutions include a few of our state schools and universities. Te Piringa Faculty of Law at the University of Waikato is committed to ensuring that tikanga and treaty understanding are woven through all levels of its curriculum. There is no quota system, but approximately 30 per cent of the students are Māori. The University of Canterbury claims to be the first 'treaty university', with a treaty partnership office, based in Kā Waimaero, the Ngāi Tahu Research Centre, which is headed by Ngāi Tūāhuriri ūpoko and Associate Professor Te Maire Tau. He says Canterbury is the first university to embed mana whenua into its structure of the university and describes his role as working alongside the vice-chancellor to include te ao Māori and matauranga and uphold the treaty in all decision making.

These are bold initiatives but they don't have power sharing enshrined in their founding constitutions. And there are critics from within the Māori world who dismiss them as 'flogging a dead horse', to use the words of Hemopereki Simon's opinion column in the *New Zealand Herald* two days after the Canterbury announcement in September 2021. As he put it bluntly on Twitter, 'Biculturalism is a Zombie concept. It is settler colonial and neoliberal. Need to create new framework.' It won't satisfy Simon, but it could be said that the education sector has all roads on offer: institutions controlled by Māori, from kōhanga reo to kura kuapapa to wānanga (offering over 100 study locations and four established campuses providing both on site and on line courses), through to charter schools, academies within high schools, to Pākehā-led ventures where Māori power sharing and decision making shape part but not all of the syllabus.

* * *

Our museums and art galleries offer an equally mixed bag of bicultural partnerships. One of the most innovative, found on the main street of Foxton, was built by the tangata whenua, the local Dutch community and the Horowhenua District Council. Te Awahou Nieuwe Stroom, which opened in 2017, offers state-of-the-art storytelling about the meeting of Dutch and Māori heritages. The language used is full of words like 'entwining' and 'inspiring'. The Piriharakeke Generation Inspiration Centre tells the story of Ngāti Raukawa ki te Tonga, alongside the Oranjehof Dutch Connection Centre, complete with a windmill, wooden clogs and decorated bikes. If the Dutch once resented being called 'the invisible immigrants', they make up for lost time in this museum. The term Pākehā doesn't feature here. So does that make the bicultural label redundant or simply add to the complications that Pākehā with a hyphen always produces? What happens if the term isn't embraced but largely ignored altogether?

The Museum of New Zealand Te Papa Tongarewa is the biggest, one of the bravest and certainly the best known internationally of all our experiments in bicultural partnership. Opened in 1998, it drew two million visitors in its first year, exceeding its annual target in the first three months. The Anglican Church's even more radical model of biculturalism six years before had provoked the wrath of the *Holmes Show* but was otherwise largely ignored by the media. Te Papa was embraced, well marketed and delighted in being at home in popular culture even more than the rarefied air of high-end museums and art galleries.

The other feature of Te Papa's achievement, compared with the church's, was its determination to translate bicultural ideas into bicultural experiences, anchored in places and things, images and sounds. Anglicans still do things mostly separately, each in their own tikanga. Visitors to Te Papa are engaged cross-culturally as soon as they walk through the door, just as they have been from the day it was declared open by a Pākehā girl and a Māori boy holding hands with yachtsman Sir Peter Blake. Ngāti Porou elder, Dr Api Mahuika, who chaired the Māori advisory committee, Ngāi Kaiwawao, understood the difference it made for Māori to be actively involved in the physical things and everything about the museum from the start – its architecture, management, the nature and nurture of collections, the visitor experience and the care of the things displayed.

The museum's marae, Rongomaraeroa, was central to the kaupapa of Te Papa. Traditionally marae are places not only for welcoming, meeting and mourning but also for eating and sleeping. Māori and Pākehā sometimes had different versions of what this particular marae could be. Ken Gorbey, who played a key role in shaping the visitor experience at Te Papa, wanted the marae to be a central forum space, having been inspired by a chapel-like space of artwork and architecture that he'd seen, not in Aotearoa but in Mexico City.

Rongomaraeroa was to be a marae for all people but, as the museum's first kaihautū (Māori co-leader) Cliff Whiting said, it was important that this happened without compromising its Māori protocols. The original purpose was to give Māori an appropriate way to address their taonga in Te Papa. Although it 'might not be that real for Pākehā', Rongomaraeroa would still give all New Zealanders a central and unifying place to stand. So Pākehā settler stories are incorporated into the wharenui itself, the house within the house. It was Whiting's vision and collaborative approach that created this space, now regarded as Aotearoa's national marae, weaving the traditional and contemporary together, decorated in modern pastel colours, carrying the story of Tāne separating earth and sky and bringing light to the world.

Stories of that sort of interaction abound in Te Papa's origins. *Te Māori* travelling to the Metropolitan Museum in New York in 1984 was the first game changer, not only for the international attention it received, but also for the huge admiration it enjoyed at home, especially during the national tour it made as *Te Hokinga Mai*, the return home. The timing was perfect, as Māori looked for expression of their newly restored role as cultural leaders and Pākehā were discovering an identity not dependent on Europe.

Then there was an array of leaders with the vision and nerve to make things happen. Sir Peter Tapsell, as Minister of Internal Affairs, was very clear about the role of Māori as tangata whenua. Ken Gorbey came from a successful career working closely with Tainui to establish the Waikato Museum and brought his training as a Pākehā partner. Dr Api Mahuika ensured the Māori voice from across the country was always central, even to the choosing of the institution's name. He played a charismatic role. Former Prime Minister Bill Rowling chaired the Project Development Board and later the Te Papa Board and was a crucial voice in ensuring government support for the project. He maintained a clear and methodical lead, even when the bicultural focus blurred around the board table. It was hard work at the start. Despite the influence of Māori leaders, the early governance structure was monocultural in its approach. Chief Executive Cheryll Sotheran worked to change that, convincing Cliff Whiting to join and become kaihautū, and with her lead the staff.

Gorbey tells a lovely story, in his book *Te Papa to Berlin*, which illustrates the kind of chemistry that grew between these leaders. Rowling died before the museum opened. A relocated pōhutukawa tree was to honour his memory but things became complicated when an electrical cable was found entwined in the tree roots. It was finally freed, risky though it was, and moved, replanted then nearly died when its roots were waterlogged. Eventually the tree flourished. Whiting and his elders who followed this journey throughout believed the success was a sign of good things to come. The pōhutukawa, named 'the troublesome one' by Whiting, was 'a sign that Rowling had not yet left us'.

Clarity about the founding concept is the other part of Te Papa's bicultural success. It must be a place for all New Zealanders. It must tell our stories. It must be bicultural, sharing the governance, required by the treaty, between the tangata whenua and the other peoples of New Zealand. The management structure tried to address the necessary power sharing in the relationship between the CEO and the kaihautū. That has swayed over the years depending on the personalities involved and the changing lines of reporting directly or indirectly to the governing board. But at a deeper level, just who were these two partners in this bicultural relationship? No doubt about what tangata whenua means, and under Mahuika's leadership that voice was constantly tested across the iwi. But what did Te Papa understand as the other partner?

As Gorbey makes clear, the name Pākehā wasn't an option. It was too European in its connection, just as tauiwi was too foreign and non-Māori too negative. He argued that New Zealand is a pluralistic society and it is just 'too authoritarian to demand that New Zealanders from India or the Pacific Islands or anywhere else must become Pākehā just to be part of Our Place (Te Papa)'. Judge Eddie Durie's suggestion was favoured: tangata tiriti, those who belong to the land by right of the Treaty of Waitangi.

Jock Phillips, who was contracted to develop Te Papa's history exhibitions, held a similar position. 'The question of what is pākehā history is of course a major conceptual issue, but at an operational level, we solved the matter quickly. We argued that there was no pākehā identity as such. Pākehā had co-opted an identity as New Zealanders and their definition as we quickly discovered included Māori. So the exhibitions became New

Zealand identity from a pākehā perspective.' It is a little startling to me that our premiere showcase of national identity believes there is no such thing as Pākehā identity. But that points to the depth of the dilemma we face as those who are not Māori but seek to belong here and find a name to be known by.

So how does Te Papa manage to address the heritage of being Pākehā, even though that might be only a part of the experience of living here not as Māori? It goes to some lengths to avoid that question. It's distinctly uneasy in making too much of the colonial history of Māori and Pākehā interaction and conflict, the legacy of racism and the continuing inequality. By overlooking or downplaying that ugly side of our story, stereotypes are reinforced of a unified Māori culture pitted against a silent and guilty Pākehā one. The introduction of a New Zealand history curriculum will gradually have its influence and make it easier to present a more complete account of the story we share, for better or worse. Until then Te Papa treads carefully, not least because it is a state institution, seen to be giving the official version of our shared history. It tells our story in pieces, understandably for practical reasons, in iwi and community (settler) segments, but the sharp edges are often smoothed, and not often confronting.

* * *

Displaying the ugly side of colonialism in art galleries or museums across the country is seldom done in any consistent way, though some have tried. In 2001, for example, there was the exhibition *Parihaka: The Art of Passive Resistance* at Wellington's City

Gallery. Puke Ariki in New Plymouth has offered some frank displays on the same story, all the more powerful for drawing on local knowledge. Generally, however, the approach is still largely based on the display of objects rather than storytelling. Part of the problem is the lack of research and scholarship on the subject and iwi, naturally, are more likely to focus on what happened to their ancestors rather than the country as a whole. They do not want to be seen as victims and there is an emphasis in many museums on showing the resurgence of Māori identity and on celebrating achievements.

Auckland University sociologist Avril Bell, one of the clearest academic voices in this debate, tells a story that illustrates this sensitivity. A work by Charles Goldie, famous for his paintings of Māori elders at the turn of the twentieth century, was exhibited at Te Papa in 2002. The painting's original title, *Darby and Joan*, from the English proverbial phrase for an elderly couple's long romance, referred to the attachment between the woman and the carved figure. It was similar to other nostalgic titles Goldie used, fitting the belief, common at the time, that Māori were doomed to extinction and Pākehā, in the infamous words of politician Dr Isaac Featherston, must 'smooth the pillow of a dying race' as Māori died through dispossession and disease.

Presumably to avoid offending Māori viewers, the title was removed and replaced with the subject's name, Ina Te Papatahi, and her iwi, but the accompanying caption had a coy twist. Headed 'Smoothing whose pillow?', it noted the 'erroneous belief that Māori were a dying race' and went on: 'Whether Goldie himself believed this is not clear. What is clear is that his fame would soon be "smoothed" by the arrival of modern ideas about art.' So take that, Mr Goldie. A more robust form of biculturalism might have been less eager to put the artists in his place and addressed the ambiguous but overwhelming conviction of that Māori were about to disappear – ambiguous because it was not all about racist Pākehā with no interest in Māori well-being. The grandfather of a good Pākehā friend of mine devoted years of his life to learning and practising the traditional but rapidly disappearing skills of Māori carving and adorning a local church in Canterbury with his work, afraid that such carving would otherwise disappear without trace.

Ken Gorbey believes it's time for Te Papa to 'abandon the current exhibition territories, which have outlived their purpose, and use Our Place, coupled with the idea of standing together on and with this island nation, tūrangawaewae, as the basis for the new'. But that would be a step too far and far too soon for most people. Many Māori would say there's still too much work to be done in restoring equity. Many Pākehā would say, 'Okay, let's get on with it. Skip the past and grab the future.' There's something visionary, though, about Gorbey's call. Maybe places like Te Papa should be set aside for dreaming of what might be for a once and future Aotearoa.

* * *

Although conservation of the things that shape our heritage is important, equally crucial for our bicultural future is the conservation of the natural landscape. Our monocultural institutions, agencies and government departments haven't done well on that score; hence the slow shift towards bicultural models of governance over parks, lakes and rivers. To achieve that has required some ground-breaking shifts in legislation, none bigger than the 2014 Te Urewera Act which, for the first time in our history, withdrew the status of national park, managed by the Department of Conservation, and turned the region into a legal entity 'with all the rights, powers, duties and liabilities of a legal person'. The board appointed to manage the park was made up of equal numbers of Tūhoe and Crown representatives for the first three years, with the ratio of new appointments then to shift in favour of Tūhoe. Board decisions are to reflect Tūhoe customary values and law, concepts such as rāhui. Resource consents are not required for work in the park. Even more startling, the act declared the mountainous bush-clad region, with Lake Waikaremoana at its heart, to be 'a place of spiritual value with its own mana and mauri [spirit] … with an identity in and of itself'.

This is astonishing language for a piece of legislation. Dr Jacinta Ruru, who had researched reforming the ownership and management of national parks, had dreamt of radical legislative change in New Zealand, but not that it would come so soon. She quoted then Minister of Conservation Nick Smith speaking during the third reading of the bill: 'If you had told me 15 years ago that Parliament would almost unanimously be able to agree to this bill, I would have said, "You're dreaming, mate." It has been a real journey for New Zealand, iwi, and Parliament to get used to the idea that Māori are perfectly capable of conserving New Zealand treasures at least as well as Pākehā and departments of State.' DOC has not yet managed to deliver on what the Act envisaged to address the Crown's legacy of neglect for Te Urewera. Tūhoe has attempted to host visitors in their accustomed manner but this is not sustainable with the existing resources. So the partnership is still sorting itself out but the achievement of reaching agreement for the long term is still remarkable.

Three years after the Te Urewera Act, the Te Awa Tupua (Whanganui River Claims Settlement) Act 2017 was equally ground-breaking. This extraordinary legislation gave effect to Ruruku Whakatupua, the Whanganui River Deed of Settlement, with redress of $80 million, which had been signed in 2014, ending the country's longest running litigation over its longest navigable river. The spirit of the agreement was captured on the opening page in the frequently quoted words:

> *E rere kau mai te awa nui*
> *mai i te kahui maunga ki Tangaroa*
> *Ko au te awa*
> *Ko te awa ko au.*

> *The river flows*
> *From the mountains to the sea*
> *I am the river*
> *The river is me.*

The whole 290-kilometre length of the river, from the mountains to the ocean, is recognised as a legal entity, Te Awa Tupua, incorporating all its tributaries and all its 'physical and metaphysical elements as an indivisible and living whole'.

Māori had no difficulty in understanding the import of that. For many Pākehā, however, to imagine a river taking on the status of a person was an even bigger stretch than the Urewera settlement. Treaty Settlements Minister Chris Finlayson understood that challenge. 'I know the natural inclination of some people is to say it's pretty strange to give a natural resource a legal personality,' he told the *New Zealand Herald* at the time. 'But it's no stranger than family trusts or companies or incorporated societies.' His reassurance wouldn't have convinced everyone. But the comparison he made didn't address the great gulf between the world views of the two cultures, Māori matauranga – knowledge that welds the physical and spiritual worlds seamlessly into each other – and Pākehā culture which, in its current expression at least, sees spirituality as dodgy at best.

There's a deeper dilemma at work in this standoff. It connects with Michael King's claim that Pākehā can claim to be indigenous in Aotearoa. Among the many problems that assertion created, not least the offence it created to the people who'd belonged here for rather longer, was the effect it had of cutting off Pākehā from their mostly (but not only) European countries of origin, and from where they drew their own spiritual roots. If, for example, Pākehā were still knowledgeable and proud about their Gaelic and Celtic heritages, if they were secure in the many spiritual traditions they brought with them to New Zealand, they'd have much less difficulty celebrating with Māori over the recognition of their rivers and parks. Because our ancestors had very similar understandings of the spiritual significance of the natural world. And to insist we're indigenous, like Māori, is to shut down that connection that Pākehā enjoy with earlier heritages much richer and longer and more spiritual than our still recent, hard-scrabble settler history. That history was, in fact, more about leaving behind anything that was too spiritual, let alone religious. For example, church attendance in Auckland in the 1850s was only half what it was back in England. By cutting themselves off from the spiritual traditions of their forebears, Pākehā risk leaving themselves stuttering and inarticulate when it comes to conversation with their Māori partner.

It doesn't need to be like that. Pākehā don't have to look far into their British (or any number of other) heritages to find eloquent language for understanding why the Whanganui River needs to be treated personally. This is what the most famous Romantic poet William Wordsworth wrote, not about a river, but looking down on the hillside ruins of Tintern Abbey:

> *And I have felt*
> *A presence that disturbs me with the joy*
> *Of elevated thoughts; a sense sublime*
> *Of something far more deeply interfused,*
> *Whose dwelling is the light of setting suns,*
> *And the round ocean and the living air,*

And the blue sky, and in the mind of man;
A motion and a spirit, that impels
All thinking things, all objects of all thought,
And rolls through all things.

If the site that inspired those lines was under threat from a new motorway, we'd want some legal protection to protect its importance for our culture. The challenge for Pākehā in understanding Māori spirituality lies in rediscovering their own. The sense of mystery and wonder and beauty is not copyrighted by any one culture over another but shared by all who have eyes to see.

The spirituality that is woven into the words of Te Tiriti, embedded in the language that was so carefully chosen to express the covenant being signed that day, not simply on paper, but in the hearts and souls of those present, is the same spirituality that is enshrined in the treaty settlements being made today for rivers, lakes and lands the breadth and length of Aotearoa. The spirituality Pākehā need to understand that may well be slow to surface, but it's there. They may have given up church- and temple-going as a mainstream activity but they can still respond to the sense that the natural world is telling them more than meets the eye.

PART IV

FINDING A
SHARED FUTURE

CHAPTER 23

The landscape has shifted

In 2004 David Slack wrote a book called *Bullshit, Backlash and Bleeding Hearts: A Confused Person's Guide to the Great Race Row*. When Chris Trotter reviewed it for the *Listener* he dismissed it as a less than 'even-handed attempt to understand and elucidate the Brash backlash'. Six months before the book appeared, National Party leader Don Brash had thrown incendiary words at the Orewa Rotary Club and the country. Son of a Presbyterian minister and ecumenical leader who helped to pioneer anti-racism programmes here and overseas two decades before, Brash had dismissed the Treaty of Waitangi as a 'grievance industry', accused Labour of fostering separatism, attacked public displays of Māori spirituality and labelled Māori parliamentary seats as an 'anachronism'. Slack's book, wrote Trotter, should have weighed equally arguments for and against the Brash polemic and the constitutional claims of the treaty itself. In an astonishing comparison, Trotter said, 'it's as if someone writing a book about the Iraq war confined their questioning to Bush, Cheney, Rumsfeld and Perle'.

I doubt whether such a comparison, and indeed such a review, would gain much traction today. Even less than the Iraq War, the treaty is no longer discussed in such a way. For one thing, it's widely accepted as our nation's founding document, symbolised at the centre of our national museum, and most permanent of all, enshrined in our law books, in more and more detail and frequency. Its precedents increasingly influence our legal processes, drawing on tikanga concerning everything from asset management to attitudes to death. That the appeal hearings about the Peter Ellis Christchurch Civic Creche case were able to continue after his death is a case in point. The constitutional implications of the treaty are still debated, but the validity and centrality of its existence in our national life is rarely contested.

Except perhaps on Facebook. Trotter's review appeared in the same year that Mark Zuckerberg launched Facebook in Silicon Valley. Two decades on, the impact of social media on polarising and inflaming discussion about race is all too clear. It, and other platforms such as Twitter, allow people to rant and rave and feed an army of trolls with a diet of anti-treaty and anti-Māori diatribes, anonymously and without consequences. The most dangerous and destructive segment of the bicultural debate in this country happens below the radar in this way, blind copied to protect the readers from the shame of being involved. Trotter would never be a part of that, but surprisingly there is an ageing collection of retired cabinet ministers, once prominent lawyers and journalists who are. Their views no longer make the pages of mainstream media but their Facebook blogs reinforce the prejudices of the already converted. Their recent digital arrival in cyberspace is a new and ugly feature of our landscape.

But there are many more positive new contours to this landscape that have also emerged since Brash lectured the Rotarians and Trotter wrote his review. There is now a much younger cohort, relaxed about living biculturally and hearing te reo spoken around them and on media as the new normal. A Colmar Brunton poll in December 2020 showed that eight out of every 10 New Zealanders regarded te reo as part of our national identity. Over 300 schools now offer bilingual and immersion programmes, more than 20,000 students are enrolled and the aim to have one million speakers of the language no longer looks like the pipedream it was 20 years ago. Over 50 per cent of Māori have some speaking ability in te reo and the enrolment of Pākehā learners outstrips the supply of teachers. To attempt to speak te reo, to be willing to listen to it sympathetically, even though you wish you understood a lot more, is a sure sign that the cultural climate is changing. And to the generation of primary school and increasingly secondary students for whom spoken te reo is as ordinary as a bike ride, and karakia as unsurprising as eating breakfast, the bicultural debate promises to be much easier in the future. In light of this shift, it's little wonder the Broadcasting Standards Authority has given up accepting complaints on excessive use of te reo on RNZ National.

The best thing about this ever-widening constituency of sympathy is that it dissolves the charge Trotter made, namely that books like Slack's are no more than exercises in 'elite consensus formation'. It's true that the bicultural debate in the past has felt and read like the preserve of academics, policy specialists and government report writers. But consider, in lists that are nothing like complete, institutions like Te Papa and RNZ; movies like *Dark Horse* and *Waru*; musicians like Stan Walker, Whirimako Black, Moana Maniapoto, Hinewehi Mohi, Anika Moa, Che Fu, Troy Kingi, the late Mahinārangi Tocker and Prince Tui Teka, soul singer Teeks (Te Karehana Gardiner-Toi), composer and singer Maisey Rika and sonic shaman Mara TK; artists like Ralph Hotere, Robyn Kahukiwa, Emily Karaka, Lisa Reihana, Rachel Mataira, Rachael Rakena, Peter Robinson, Reuben Paterson, Michael Parekowhai and Para Matchitt; writers like Patricia Grace, Hone Tuwhare, Witi Ihimaera, Keri Hulme, Alan Duff, Tina Makereti, Becky Manawatu, Apirana Taylor and Renée; journalists and presenters like Derek Fox, Julian Wilcox, Carol Hirschfeld, Mihingarangi Forbes, Carmen Parahi, Peata Melbourne, Shannon Haunui-Thompson, Mani Dunlop and Oriini Kaipara (the first news presenter with a moko kauae to present a mainstream television news bulletin); and columnists like Shane Te Pou, Lizzie Marvelly, Aroha Awarau, Joel Maxwell and Glenn McConnell. There's such an abundance of talent to choose from that it's hard to know where to start or end. All have broken open the bicultural debate by converting it into the currency of popular culture.

The presence of 29 Māori politicians in Parliament, more than ever before, making up almost a quarter of the House, has also helped to make the debate accessible. They have changed the look of the place too: Foreign Minister Nanaia Mahuta has a moko kauae; Rawiri Waititi, co-leader of Te Pāti Māori, has a full facial moko and is Stetson hatted to honour the C Company soldiers from the Māori Battalion. 'Now I know how a Pākehā feels walking onto a marae,' he said, on arriving in Parliament. The bicultural debate is everywhere on display and within reach, helped along by a few TV ads like the Mitre 10 guy who shows his bumbling Pākehā customer the tools to buy that won't risk him chopping his hand off.

Māori and Pākehā are talking to each other and laughing with, sometimes about, each other, more easily than any time since the 1830s. But the old tribes of Pākehā discontent still assemble to salute the same old flags and there are still tough things to be talked about, and huge challenges about even being able to talk to each other. You could, if you were brave enough, draw a comparison between the conversation over vaccination for Covid-19 and the one about being bicultural. Both dialogues have a hard-core constituency of people who are more defined by conspiracy theories than rational debate, and who are impressed by some dodgy science. Our bicultural history is well stocked with theories of eugenics, racial superiority, discredited ideas on intelligence and racial stereotyping. Some of these are still alive and well, despite all the evidence against them. The challenge is how to convince people that a bicultural future for Aotearoa is good for both Māori and Pākehā and all the other cultures that want to call Aotearoa Our Place.

It won't happen by yelling at or demonising each other, by labelling each other as woke liberals or reactionary bigots. Nor by whipping up Pākehā guilt for the evils of colonialism. Polarising Māori and Pākehā identity into separate, self-contained cultural enclaves set against each other is counter-productive, no longer even possible in our well-hybridised country. Punishment and ostracism for racist behaviour when it's motivated by ignorance and fear has limited effect, though lines have to be drawn around hate speech and online abuse.

The criticism of Covid-19 vaccine and testing rollout in some Māori and Pasifika communities was all about the failure of our public health systems and communication channels to start with, rather than adding on later, a Māori or Polynesian way of doing things. In times of crisis, Pākehā still seem to believe that all cultures will and should revert to fitting into the same slot to get the job done. The same way of sending and receiving messages, on the same devices, to assemble at the same places on the same timetable – it's all equally accessible, if only we all try hard enough. There was no acknowledgement of alienation from and distrust of a health system not speaking to other cultures. Only when infection rates were too high and vaccination numbers too low was it understood that those who were anxious and hesitant needed to see people they trusted, speaking a language they knew, appealing to their dignity, their families and their own self-interest and well-being, without threat or bullying or talking down.

Over the summer of 2021–22 there was sharp criticism of the potentially devastating consequences of government decisions and failure to communicate. Writing in *Metro* in the summer of 2022, Miriama Aoake argued that 'either directly or indirectly through neglect, the Crown has been trying to kill us since 1840' and by opening the Auckland borders on 15 December, 'the government [had] effectively condemned whānau to die'. The Waitangi Tribunal, which held an urgent hearing in December, said something similar, albeit in more restrained language, in a strongly critical report later that month. Treaty principles of active protection and equity had been breached. The accusation of personal racism is the most loaded line in the Kiwi vocabulary. Institutional racism, embedded in our history and official policy making, is hard enough to own and cope with. But we can and must because the evidence is overwhelming. You can say to someone, 'I think you and I have inherited and are still entangled in a web of structured racism', and be able to keep talking. But to accuse someone personally of being a racist is a different story. It has the same effect as calling him or her scum, inhuman, rotten, even evil.

Some, though, wear that racist label deliberately, even proudly, as a chosen and deliberate attitude aimed at those less powerful and privileged. They fill the pages of Alt Right and conspiracy-driven websites, shout racist insults at sporting events and protest marches. They must be named and shamed. But there are others who give racist offence out of ignorance, misguided belief, years of being surrounded by people who think it's okay, even funny. Getting such people to change is more about education than accusation and shaming, helping them see the destructive effect of their words.

To be branded racist is the ultimate insult in a country that prides itself on being egalitarian, a place where we like to think everyone gets, if not a bargain, then certainly a fair go. Where personal racism is evident, it needs to be confronted, not by assumptions about motivation, but descriptions of observed behaviour, fed back by a trusted person with an invitation to consider the effect it might be having.

It's easy to colour our history white with racism to explain past wrongs, but it's much harder to find effective ways to change that legacy. The racism tag can become a recipe for paralysis and resentment. Pākehā won't join the bicultural journey until they see it's as good for them as it is for Māori.

* * *

But there's another volatile issue that must be tackled. Until the mid-twentieth century, 'colonial' was a neutral word in the Pākehā vocabulary, when it was used at all. The colonial era was way back then, when Pākehā forebears lived simply, worked hard, dressed quaintly, still went to church and ate big Sunday dinners of stuffed mutton, weirdly known as colonial goose. Then, after the Second World War, New Zealanders who were not Māori started to discover a Pākehā settler as opposed to a European migrant identity and culture, with its own songs and art and sport. Rugby became the heavy truck to carry that identity to beat England, not imitate it. And visiting Poms helped to show them how different they had become – in Austin Mitchell's famous words, citizens of a half-gallon, quarter-acre, pavlova paradise. Britain joining the European Union and ending its reliance on our frozen lamb and butter only served to confirm that severance. 'Colonial' became a term that Pākehā were well on the way to getting rid of – until Māori made it a dirty word.

Reinforced by an international movement against colonisation, Māori redefined the word and reapplied it to Pākehā in a whole new way. The word they thought they had shrugged off and dumped in the dustbin of history was now used to describe them as the uninvited invaders and greedy exploiters who signed a treaty, then ignored it, who drummed up wars then punished Māori for fighting them. The colonial heritage, once quaint, then discarded, has been reinstated as the centrepiece of the bicultural debate. And piece by treaty settlement piece, apology by apology, reparation payment and return of land, the Crown struggles to right the injustices of the colonial past.

Decolonisation has become the agenda that drives the debate, good for Māori and necessary for Pākehā. And that creates unease in the Pākehā camp, for many who don't know too much about this country's history and aren't convinced that the era was as bad as it sounds. As Moana Jackson puts it, 'colonisation has been rebranded not as a violent home invasion but a grand if sometimes flawed adventure that was somehow "better than" anywhere else because of the proclaimed honour of the Crown in treaty making'. He wonders whether 'colonisation is an injustice that is often too painful to be fully told'.

His fear is based on just how hard it will be for many Pākehā to retell the story of their colonial past, which betrayed the interdependence signed up to in the treaty, then replaced it with a narrative of supremacy. Māori have told Pākehā that, but until they take hold of their story, own and reshape it, it will remain too hard to handle.

That is what's at stake in the reform of the history teaching in our schools, in the renaming of our signs and names and monuments, in the return of confiscated lands and taonga. Every redress made, every honest retelling of what happened, will help Pākehā like me to leave behind the fantasies they grew up with of a Better Britain in the South Seas providing mutton and soldiers for the empire, while enjoying the gratitude of the natives. Until those fantasies are gone, I can't discover and enjoy the parts of that colonial heritage that I can be proud to own: the incredible work ethic, ingenuity and resilience of my grandparents and great-grandparents, the brave and faithful way they stood by their children in times of depression and trouble, their service to the country in wars they didn't choose, their generosity and sacrifice in building community and overcoming isolation.

Jackson suggests the way ahead might not be so much about decolonisation as an 'ethic of restoration', whereby we all work on finding the truth about our part of the story.

That would involve rebalancing and rebuilding relationships between the cultures, restoring their independence and, in his words, 'rekindling faith in the "ought to be" in this land; to draw upon the same land-and-tikanga centred way of ordering society that was envisaged in Te Tiriti.'

How we talk about each other and hear each other's stories will make or break our bicultural future. It will do what Ngāti Kahungungu call mahi tūhono – the work that brings people together. Jackson lists the qualities that this restoration work involves: the values of place and protecting the land, of tikanga that shape how we ought to be living here, of community and belonging and balance in relationships, and of conciliation building a consensual democracy. There's nothing threatening about that list, nothing that isn't as good for Pākehā as it is for Māori.

CHAPTER 24

Aotearoa as it just might be

The Covid-19 pandemic, and its even more overwhelming partner, climate change, have shrunk our appetite for second-guessing the future. But looking ahead and imagining a better future for all of us in Aotearoa is still necessary, even if we're just lighting one candle at a time. And, happily, it's a guessing game that we should expect to see played more and more, especially as the 2040 deadline rolls closer. The 200th anniversary of the signing of Te Tiriti o Waitangi carries some special heft – long enough to put up or shut up about how serious both parties were; close enough now to see and feel the difference the changes being made. The 2040 target means the document can't be kicked into touch again as it has been so often before.

But just what 2040 will look like for impatient Māori and anxious Pākehā is a work in progress, led by the government commissioning of the report called *He Puapua*. The word means a break, usually in the waves, and refers to a sea change in our usual norms and approaches, both social and political. Commissioned as a follow-up to give some flesh to the National government's earlier ratification of the United Nations Declaration on the Rights of Indigenous Peoples, the report is a discussion document that sets out a roadmap of steps towards 2040, all awaiting government support and consultation with Māori. The hysterical reaction from right-wing think tanks and radio hosts might have left you thinking it was already official policy.

Part of the problem is to do with language. The bicultural journey is saddled with abstract and general talk about participation and inclusion, justice, equality and equity. Much of the time it's more about reassuring each other that we're all doing the right thing together – comfort words, even self-promoting words. To spell out what equity might mean in the same sentence would spoil it all because you'd have to say what you were willing to give up and let go of, by which date, and name the people you'd need to work with but would rather not.

He Puapua begins by reassuring readers that it respects the government's priorities of 'well-being and economic inclusivity' as well as the rights and interests of the disabled, women, elderly, youth, children and LGBTQI+ communities, all of which must be front and centre. And that's only the introduction. Any Pākehā reader anxious about our bicultural future, unconfident about how to operate in that space between the cultures, threatened by the language and demands of Māori for recognition, is going to run for cover before reading further. But if you look at it calmly, *He Puapua* offers a vision of what 2040 might look like, based on five principles, all of which are extensions of what is already happening: rangatiratanga giving Māori authority over

Māori matters and jurisdiction over their lands and resources; kāwanatanga or governance, whereby Māori share in central and local government; the continued return of Crown but not private land; Māori authority over their culture and language; and equity to ensure Māori are thriving and prosperous.

There are other voices singing songs about 2040, some of them more radical but none attracting the same fear and loathing as *He Puapua*. In 2019, for example, there was the *Ināia Tonu Nei* report, which summarised a hui held in Rotorua to discuss justice reform for Māori. 'Now is the time; we lead, you follow' was the title theme of the weekend, which addressed the frustration felt by Māori at a larger summit convened the year before by the minister of justice. The Rotorua hui made it clear that reform of the justice system must be led by Māori ways of seeing and knowing, working to rebalance disruption to wellness, health and well-being. Its suggestion that prisons should be abolished by 2040 goes back over decades from a range of reforming voices, liberal and conservative. Bill English back in 2011 declared the prison system a 'moral and fiscal failure'. New Zealand should never build another one, he said.

Such suggestions about the future haven't been popular with the major political parties. They're seen as a diversion from the serious business of government and best left to fringe groups who will never get the chance to realise them. Some of the best ideas remain in the parking lot. For example, The Opportunities Party (TOP) has a brave wish list for a change in paid work, which could be smarter, more technologically and digitally based, using 3D printing. TOP also wants to see domestic violence, child uplifts and prison populations down to the OECD average, fossil fuel use cut by two-thirds, an education system focused on producing transferable skills rather than test results ... Action Station, a crowd-funded, community campaigning organisation, claims 180,000 supporters, and assembles its vision for our future from extensive surveys and face-to-face meetings through dinner parties. It's produced *Te Ira Tāngata: a People's Agenda for Aoteroa New Zealand*, which proposes a guaranteed minimum income, a 1 per cent wealth tax, zero carbon and a low cap on political donations.

And there are some 2040 targets already set by government policy, including a million te reo speakers and a predator-free countryside. But unlike *He Puapua*, which dares to offer a timeline and a roadmap of how to get there, many of the 2040 dreams are aspirational only. What might some of these next steps look like, set out more modestly?

* * *

The challenge today is to find a new normal that is not either/or but a partnership between tangata whenua and tangata tiriti, embracing all who make their home here. For all the current backbiting, fearmongering and stalling, there is every reason to believe New Zealanders will enjoy the bicultural future this book explores. And Pākehā will get there by being nudged and pushed, and by dreaming. The nudging and pushing will come from the shifting landscape that they will have to accept, as surely as the new constraints on everyone's lives caused by Covid-19 and climate change. The move for Māori to govern things Māori is now hardwired and irreversible. So is the move for them to share in governing the things that affect us both. Shared governance becomes a matter of life and death for everyone. We're only as safe as the most marginal in our midst. Healthcare that protects just some of us isn't going to work for any of us, eventually. Indiscriminate viruses will see to that.

Pākehā are also going to be nudged into this bicultural future by the law, because increasingly Māori rely on the law to reach their goals. When Dame Tureiti Moxon's people began their treaty settlement claim on the Mohaka River, they lacked access to legal counsel. So she went out and gained a law degree to help make it happen. As it did. Māori faith in the law exceeds that of most Pākehā. They trust it to work, even though it has failed them so often. Te Kooti's words are often quoted: 'Ka kuhu au ki te ture, hei matua mō te pani' – I seek refuge in the law, for it is the parent of the oppressed. Joe Williams, the first Māori to be appointed as a judge to the Supreme Court, has said that his inspiration came from this 'great kōrero'. Because Māori look to the law as a last resort, there was considerable concern when the right of appeal to the Privy Council was abolished and replaced by the Supreme Court.

The treaty is yet to be enshrined in law with independent legal status, though it is entwined in the statute books, referred to in more than 60 separate Acts of Parliament. Faith in workable laws slowly increases for many Māori – many but not all. There is an intense debate in legal academic circles about how far judges in our state courts should be deciding on the meaning of tikanga and matauranga. Some scholars warn that biculturalism in law, given the colonial history that shaped our legal system, could limit Māori claims to rangatiratanga as a domain for Māori to devolve to other Māori.

Other voices, Pākehā rather than Māori, and often from right-wing media rather than the law, fear that this Māori faith in the law is being used to dominate or disenfranchise Pākehā, leaving them short-changed when it comes to basic rights. But is that fear warranted? Joe Williams describes what is really at stake here. 'To our people in 1840, the idea of a text-related contractual relationship was utterly foreign. For them then, as now, the transaction was … all about relationships.' They wanted 'a mutually sustaining relationship where they kept their mana and got all the advantages of the Pākehā world. There were considerable advantages they already knew about, in return for letting Pākehā come. And we wanted it to enhance our mana and enhance theirs. And we usually gave effect to that by swapping DNA. Almost always.'

It all comes down to relationship, which has to be built through shared contact, walking alongside, listening, waiting, giving time and resources, winning respect and trust. Williams calls those relationships horizontal – communities working side by side, rather than vertical, and he sees them growing by the day, building mutual advantage for both partners. 'Iwi are starting to impose requirements on a Crown that needs the partnership as much as the iwi do, to solve problems that the Crown no longer has the ability to solve.' Such equal horizontal relationships require trust from both cultures, something that's eroded by every accusatory headline and social media slanging match. And it takes Pākehā standing back and getting out of the way when Māori ask for space and resources to get things done, after years of vertical relationships – where things have been done for them – have failed to deliver.

Where partnerships do work, what sociologist Robert Pitman calls a 'social capital' is built up for both cultures. Like money in a bank account, it gathers interest and value for both partners and reaps a harvest of mutual goodwill. The All Blacks at their best have done that, as have such figures such as Dame Kiri Te Kanawa and Sir Howard Morrison, and filmmakers like Taika Waititi and Dame Jane Campion. These people are honoured because they're our social capitalists, for Pākehā as much as Māori. We dare to invest our trust in a shared future because of them.

That future is made possible not only by capital but also by connections. Whakapapa is the word, and whanaungatanga, the familial bonds and networks that bind the Māori world together. And because they are bonds that hold Pākehā as well, these can be words for all New Zealanders to speak. Pepeha is the word for the speech you give to introduce yourself to a new gathering. You say how you arrived here, the places you come from and the families you belong to, name the mountain and the river that define where you belong. But then you look around the room to see what connections you can make with others and share the stories that link you. You describe your entanglements. Everyone can do that, whether you arrived 150 years ago on a sailing ship or last month on a 767.

The spirituality bound up in whakapapa is the most accessible part of te ao Māori to Pākehā with their own interest in studying genealogy. It doesn't take any great leap of imagination for us to understand the Māori world view as a vast network of kinship, as Dame Anne Salmond has described it, where ancestors remain active in the world, still in touch with their descendants, and kinship is related not only to humans but also 'to all forms of life from the first surge of energy ... till earth and sky emerge then ancestors of animals, plants and people'. Anyone who has read the Book of Genesis in the Bible won't have too much trouble with that.

Former lawyer and now UK-based performance coach Owen Eastwood, who has Ngāi Tahu ancestry, has applied the whakapapa concept to his successful work with the English football team. As he details in *Belonging: The Ancient Code of Togetherness*, given his players' disparate racial, religious and football club backgrounds, Eastwood worked at building a shared culture that created a sense of belonging for everyone involved, even before they got immersed in game tactics and strategies. For him, whakapapa is 'not only a way to understand the people who came before us and the moment we're in right now but also those who come after us and in a very natural, organic way, it became central to the work I do'.

The very idea of the treaty as a founding covenant for the nation relies on spiritual respect. That's how Māori have seen it from the beginning. That's how they still see it. In the same way, the whole debate about decolonisation relies on acknowledging a spiritual dimension. And far from being some sort of spiritual froth, it's a mammoth undertaking. We've never had anything like South Africa's Truth and Reconciliation Commission to help us do that. Maybe we need something on that scale, a sort of expanded Waitangi Tribunal with an agenda of changing hearts and souls as well as laws and title deeds. To help it along, it would require a Pākehā spirituality that was open ended, not dogmatic about any belief, willing to value material things as signs of a deeper, wider reality. It would be always looking for the underlying connections between all living things. It would be driven by a passion for justice and the fair sharing of resources. At the very least, let's settle for a respectful silence on bicultural occasions, because the spiritual framing of everything in the Māori world isn't going to go away, and to ignore it or treat it lightly or insult it as superstition, is only going to widen the gulf between the cultures. When Pākehā make an effort to start learning te reo, however ineptly or hesitantly, this spiritual dimension to the language is constantly present, built into the meaning and the sound of words.

Then there's the matter of settling on a name. New Zealander won't work, nor non-Māori. Tangata tiriti is pretty useful. Colonist used to be okay but is now acceptable only for plans to live on Mars or the moon. Pioneer is hardly ever used in New

Zealand. Maybe it sets a tone that's too brave, even laudatory. Settler carries some of that old colonial ambivalence, and a whiff of the temporary if you've watched too many Westerns with wagons rolling through, though Te Papa tries to make it work. What's more, settler is all about landholding, so it's not much use for someone who rents in the middle of Auckland and will never be able to afford a house. Ngāti Pākehā is another option. It's a description claimed by people who want to express solidarity with Māori but who haven't always worked that through with Māori and gained the permission needed to describe themselves with a Māori word. If Pākehā is a gifted term, then Ngāti is equally, if not more, so. In an increasingly multicultural society, the word Pākehā demands some sort of hyphen to go with it because the European heritage association won't go away. We may need a new word altogether if this bicultural journey is going to keep accelerating towards 2040 and beyond.

Tangata tiriti came to us from Māori, as did Pākehā in the beginning. Maybe they've got another one tucked away in a kete somewhere. Maybe we'll be known in future as they are known, more by regional names than one single national name. To be Ngāti Porou or Tūhoe or Ngāi Tahu comes before being Māori in day-to-day living. And generalisations about Māori spirituality and tikanga are treated more cautiously by Māori than by Pākehā. As Tūhoe scholar, government adviser and orator John Rangihau told Michael King back in 1985, 'I can't go around saying that because I'm Māori that Māoritanga means this and all Māori will have to follow me.'

That same diversity is found in the Pākehā world. The way Pākehā relate to Māori, express their respect for them, get invited to their gatherings, exchange words in te reo will be hugely different if they live in Gisborne rather than Geraldine, Featherston rather than Whangarei. Just as Māori is too broad a word to do justice to all the iwi and hapū it embraces, Pākehā is unable to describe the complexities of belonging here as someone who is not Māori, but knows no other home. The future will require Pākehā to be more creative about saying who they are. Maybe, with Māori help, they'll find another word or set of words to describe them region by region as Māori describe themselves iwi by iwi.

And how about a local covenant to go with the new name or names? An agreement, a mini-treaty, between the people of that place, both tangata tiriti as well as the other names they give each other, spelling out how they agree to live together, side by side. The list might include the signs that welcome and farewell, historic names they want to keep, or are willing to consider changing, directions about conservation areas, historic sites, memorials, festivals, contact people to call when things go wrong and racial tensions flare. Maybe there would need to be a whole range of these regional covenants across the country, all under the umbrella of the treaty, forged by mana whenua and tangata tiriti, known locally by all sorts of names, depending on the history and ethnic flavour of the settler people. Such covenants might not restore the harmony we saw in the Kaipara chiefs calling their white neighbours 'our beloved friends', but they might lighten the tone and language of the bicultural debate.

The two cultures also need a story to explain ourselves to each other. Māori have plenty of those. Pākehā call them myths and legends, using secular words and mindsets to explain them, missing the point in the process. But they need myths and legends just as much, and Māori ones aren't theirs to appropriate. Some Pākehā founding stories reach back into European history, and increasingly Asian and African as well, but much of the Pākehā narrative took place right here, not so long ago, for better or worse, for richer and richer, much of it greedy as colonists and settlers, but not all of it bad. It's a story that needs to be decolonised so it can be owned and embraced, rectified where possible, apologised for where necessary and even, one day, celebrated – and with eyes wide open, not half closed, to what happened. In Judge Joe Williams' words, 'Both sides have to decolonise their minds because both sides are colonised. Both sides are saying now, "We want to do it a different way." It's no longer right to say, "Evil, nasty Crown, good angel iwi," it's not like that at all.' To achieve that decolonising, that restoring, Pākehā have to start believing they can be free from all the guilt and angst that flow from denying and pretending that their history didn't happen and the treaty wasn't really sincere.

Life for Pākehā in Aotearoa would be very different if they were clear about what to call themselves, about the promises they've made to their treaty partner and the stories about their past that they're proud to tell in the presence of Māori.

There would be an end to the back-footed defensiveness that currently plagues the Pākehā persona and tips so often into anxiety and anger. Pākehā don't have a Great Trek journey like the South Africans, or a Red Sea opening to escape from Egypt like the Jews, or a Wild West wagon train ride like the Americans. Gallipoli is the nearest they get, even though it was a military defeat and, what's more, they have to share it with the Australians. Pākehā narratives aren't heroic enough for the big screen, but there are lots of smaller stories that make for more modest but still great viewing. And when Pākehā find the stories they can tell proudly, especially in the presence of Māori, eventually the stories about living in Aotearoa will be shared, with a bilingual soundtrack.

As the reaction to *He Puapua* shows, we aren't going to get there as a bicultural nation if we rely solely on writing reports about each other, getting angry about them and then rewriting them over and over again. We're going to get there by playing, praying and, yes, sleeping with each other – and there's always been a lot of that going on – and telling stories, some of them about the way we looked after each other (and there are some) when we needed a neighbour in the hard times. Sydney Carter wrote a lovely song about that: 'When I needed a neighbour, were you there?' Regardless of creed or colour or name, were you available when you were needed?

The journey to 2040 is going to be tough, not least because the global threats of climate change, pandemics and ideological culture wars and hate speech online could easily overwhelm our quest for a just bicultural future. And we have to turn around the disproportionate figures on healthcare and poverty. There is some cause, though, for hope in the rising rates of Māori educational achievement, skilled leadership, corporate wealth and even lowered prison numbers. Judge Williams points out that the generation of Māori born after 1990 are not going to jail at anything like the rate their fathers did.

Our best hope is to keep up our dreaming, along with our problem solving and legislating, and to keep talking to each other more than we do. Because it's the stuff of dreams, the meeting of imaginations, the entwining of art and music and images, the language of symbols, that's going to bring Māori and Pākehā together as much as rebalancing budgets and passing new laws. We need enough forums, meeting places, performance stages, churches, sporting events, music and art venues that make bicultural and multicultural engagement the norm rather than the exception. Not to mention more and more bicultural relationships and marriages. It will also be helped along by the growing use of te reo in greetings, place names, music and art, all building up a shared social capital. The use of the language, even in the simplest everyday exchanges, even if we stumble and make mistakes, signals a willingness to go along on this ride toward a bicultural future, and make the rapidly growing multicultural reality so much easier to embrace.

I leave the last word to a waiata that Ngāpuhi sang when Samuel Marsden and Ruatara came to Oihi in the Bay of Islands on Christmas Day 1814. The locals knew the arrival of that

Pākehā settlement would mean their lives would never be the same, but they sang this nonetheless.

> *E! ka nukunuku: E! Ka neke neke*
> *It is moving; it is shifting*
> *Look to the open sea of Waitangi*
> *Spread before us like a shining cuckoo*
> *It is good, all is well*
> *Change is coming soon.*
> *Is on the horizon*
> *It is good, all is well,*
> *Let peace be established.*

Bibliography

Maurice Andrew, *Set in a Long Place: A Life from North to South*, Hazard Press, 1999.

John Andrews, *No Other Home Than This: A History of European New Zealanders*, Craig Potton Publishing, 2009.

Carol Archie, *Māori Sovereignty: The Pākehā Perspective*, Hodder Moa Beckett, 1995.

Tony Ballantyne, *Entanglements of Empire: Missionaries, Māori, and the Question of the Body*, Auckland University Press, 2015.

Angela Ballara, *Proud to be White? A Survey of Pākehā Prejudice in New Zealand*, Heinemann, 1986.

James Belich, *The New Zealand Wars and the Victorian Interpretation of Racial Conflict*, Penguin, 1986.

James Belich, *Replenishing the Earth: The Settler Revolution, 1783–1939*, Oxford University Press, 2009.

Judith Binney, *Redemption Songs: A Life of Te Kooti Arikirangi Te Turuki*, Auckland University Press, 1995.

Judith Binney (ed.), *The Shaping of History: Essays from the* New Zealand Journal of History, *1967–1999*, Bridget Williams Books, 2001.

Judith Binney, *The Legacy of Guilt: A Life of Thomas Kendall*, Bridget Williams Books, 2005.

Judith Binney, *Encircled Lands: Te Urewera, 1820–1921*, Bridget Williams Books, 2009.

Judith Binney and Gillian Chaplin, *Ngā Mōrehu/The Survivors: The Life Histories of Eight Māori Women*, Oxford University Press, 1986.

Chris Bourke, *Goodbye Māoriland: The Songs and Sounds of New Zealand's Great War*, Auckland University Press, 2017.

Don Brash, 'Let's teach New Zealand history', elocal magazine, 2 November 2019 (https://www.donbrash.com/elocal/lets-teach-new-zealand-history)

Ian Christensen, *Cliff Whiting: He Toi Nuku, He Toi Rangi*, He Kupenga Hao I Te Reo, 2013.

John Coley, 'Venice and grievance', *The Press*, 13 December 2000.

Allan Davidson, Stuart Lange, Peter Lineham and Adrienne Puckey (eds), *Te Rongopai 1814 'Takoto te pai!': Bicentenary Reflections on Christian Beginnings and Developments in Aotearoa New Zealand*, Anglican General Synod, 2014.

Owen Eastwood, *Belonging: The Ancient Code of Togetherness*, Hachette, 2021.

Bianca Elkington, Moana Jackson, Rebecca Kiddle, Ocean Ripeka Mercier, Mike Ross, Jennie Smeaton and Amanda Thomas, *Imagining Decolonisation*, Bridget Williams Books, 2020.

Bronwyn Elsmore, *Mana from Heaven: A Century of Māori Prophets*, Reed, 1999.

Harry Evison, *The Long Dispute: Māori Land Rights and European Colonisation in Southern New Zealand*, Canterbury University Press, 1997.

Morgan Godfery, 'Give Lorde a break: Non- Māori must speak Māori for it to survive', *The Guardian* (Australian edn), 14 September 1921.

Ken Gorbey, *Te Papa to Berlin: The Making of Two Museums*, Otago University Press, 2020.

Michael Grimshaw, Michael Grimshaw, '"I am Pākeha because I live in a Māori country": Pākehā identity and the North Island myth', posted 25 July 2017 (https://pantograph-punch.com/posts/North-Island-Myth)

Scott Hamilton, https:/odbnewsblast.com/all-the-things-michael-bassett-got-wrong-in-his-noxious-article/

Michael Harcourt, 'Teaching and learning New Zealand's difficult history of colonisation in secondary school contexts', Te Herenga Waka–Victoria University of Wellington, 2020.

Florence Harsant, *They Called Me Te Maari*, Whitcoulls, 1979.

He Puapua: Report of the Working Group on a Plan to Realise the UN Declaration on the Rights of Indigenous Peoples in Aotearoa/New Zealand, Te Puni Kōkiri, 2020.

Witi Ihimaera, *Māori* , Government Printer, Wellington, 1975.

Moana Jackson in Bianca Elkington, Moana Jackson, Rebecca Kiddle, Ocean Ripeka Mercier, Mike Ross, Jennie Smeaton and Amanda Thomas, *Imagining Decolonisation*, Bridget Williams Books, 2020.

Alison Jones, *This Pākehā Life: An Unsettled Memoir*, Bridget Williams Books, 2020.

Alison Jones and Kuni Kaa Jenkins, *Tuai: A Traveller in Two Worlds*, Bridget Williams Books, 2017.

I.H. Kawharu (ed.), *Waitangi: Māori and Pākehā Perspectives of the Treaty of Waitangi*, Oxford University Press, 1989.

Michael King, *Being Pakeha: An Encounter with New Zealand and the Maori Renaissance*, Hodder & Stoughton, 1985.

Michael King (ed.), *Pākehā: The Quest for Identity in New Zealand*, Penguin, 1991.

Michael King, *Being Pākehā Now: Reflections and Recollections of a White Native*, Penguin, 1999, 2004.

Sidney Moko Mead, *Landmarks, Bridges and Visions: Aspects of Māori Culture*, Victoria University Press, 1997.

Paul Meredith (Ngati Kaputuhi/Pākehā), 'Hybridity in the third space: Rethinking bi-cultural politics in Aotearoa/New Zealand', Te Oru Rangahau Māori Research and Development Conference, Massey University, 7–9 July 1998.

Ani Mikaere, *Colonising Myths: Māori Realities/He Rukuruku Whakaaro*, Huia Publishers, 2011.

Buddy Mikaere, *Te Maiharoa and the Promised Land*, Heinemann, 1988.

Paul Moon, *Fatal Frontiers: A New History of New Zealand in the Decade before the Treaty*, Penguin, 2006.

Raymond Nairn (ed.), *Ka Tu, Ka Oho: Visions of a Bicultural Partnership in Psychology*, New Zealand Psychological Society, 2012.

New Citizen, 31 May 1973.

Keith Newman, *Ratana Revisited: An Unfiunished Legacy*, Reed, 2006.

Keith Newman, *Bible & Treaty: Missionaries Among the Māori : A New Perspective*, Penguin, 2010.

Erik Olssen, in Michael King (ed.), *Pākehā: The Quest for Identity in New Zealand*, Penguin, 1991.

Debbie Ngarewa-Packer, *New Zealand Herald*, 27 May 2021.

Otago Daily Times, 23 March 1985.

Matenga (Jack) Rangi Papuni, *'We Answer the Call to Arms': War Experience and its Toll on the Spirituality of the Māori Soldier*, University of Auckland, 2004.

Jock Phillips, 'Our history, our selves. The historian and national identity', *New Zealand Journal of History*, vol.30, no.2, 1996.

Jock Phillips, in 'Discussion of Aotearoa's New Zealand histories: draft curriculum', posted on 16 April 2021, The New Zealand Historical Association blog (https://nzha.org.nz/discussion-of-draft-history-curriculum)

Krishna Pillai, personal correspondence and conversations.

Francis Pound, *The Invention of New Zealand: Art and National Identity 1930–1970*, Auckland University Press, 2009.

Paul Reeves in Colin James (ed.), *Building the Constitution*, Institute of Policy Studies, Victoria University of Wellington, 2000.

James Ritchie, *Becoming Bicultural*, Huia Publishers, 1992.

Anne Salmond, *Between Worlds: Early Exchanges between Māori and Europeans 1773–1815*, Penguin, 1997.

Tony Simpson, *Te Riri Pākehā: White Man's Anger*, Alister Taylor, 1979.

Evelyn Stokes, *Wiremu Tamihana, Rangitira*, Huia Publishers, 2002.

Andrew Eruera Vercoe, *Educating Jake: Pathways to Empowerment*, HarperCollins, 1998.

Wayne Youle quoted in Charlie Gates, 'Why one Kiwi artist believes "the worst thing about public art is the public part"', Stuff, 12 December 2017 (https://www.stuff.co.nz/entertainment/arts/99725217/why-one-kiwi-artist-believes-the-worst-thing-about-public-art-is-the-public-part)

Ranginui Walker, *Ōpōtoki-Mai-Tawhiti: Capital of Whakatōhea*, Penguin, 2007.

Angela Wanhalla, *Matters of the Heart: A History of Interracial Marriage in New Zealand*, Auckland University Press, 2013.

John Ward, Secretary to the New Zealand Company, *Information Relative to New Zealand: Compiled for the Use of Colonists*, 2nd edn, John W. Parker, London, 1840.

Ian Wards, *The Shadow of the Land: A Study of British Policy and Racial Conflict in New Zealand 1832–1852*, Department of Internal Affairs, 1968.

Peter Webster, *Rua and the Māori Millennium*, Victoria University Press, 1979.

Joe Williams, interview with Moana Maniapoto, E-Tangata.co.nz, 16 May 2021.

David Williams, personal correspondence.

Matthew Wright, *Two Peoples, One Land: The New Zealand Wars*, Reed, 2006.

Acknowledgements

This book has been agathering for a long time. My thanks to all those who have encouraged me to keep at it, and even those who have warned me it might be better to leave it alone. You were kind enough to keep answering my questions. I'm indebted to some very special storytellers: Krishna Pillai and, in Chapter 20, David and Tureiti Moxon, Waiora Port and Paul Bushnell. I'm also grateful to RNZ for broadcasting my several series on this topic, including *Who Wants to be a Pākehā*, and to John Taylor for asking me to prepare a seminar on *He Puapua*, which Covid cancelled. My thanks to Alex Hedley and HarperCollins for their confidence and trust in asking me to write this book, and to my editor, Anna Rogers, who has been keeping my prose out of trouble for nearly 30 years.